God & Your Stuff

The Vital Link Between Your Possessions and Your Soul

WESLEY K. WILLMER
WITH MARTYN SMITH

NAVPRESS®

BRINGING TRUTH TO LIFE

OUR GUARANTEE TO YOU

The Navigators is an international Christian organization. Our mission is to reach, disciple, and equip people to know Christ and to make Him known through successive generations. We envision multitudes of diverse people in the United States and every other nation who have a passionate love for Christ, live a lifestyle of sharing Christ's love, and multiply spiritual laborers among those without Christ.

NavPress is the publishing ministry of The Navigators. NavPress publications help believers learn biblical truth and apply what they learn to their lives and ministries. Our mission is to stimulate spiritual formation among our readers.

NAVPRESS, BRINGING TRUTH TO LIFE, and the NAVPRESS logo are registered trademarks of NavPress. Absence of ® in connection with marks of NavPress or other parties does not indicate an absence of registration of those marks.

© 2002 by Wesley K. Willmer
All rights reserved. No part of this publication may be reproduced in any form without written permission from NavPress, P.O. Box 35001, Colorado Springs, CO 80935. www.navpress.com

ISBN 1-57683-234-1

Cover design and cover illustration by David Carlson
Creative Team: David Hazard, Greg Clouse, Darla Hightower, Pat Miller

Some of the anecdotal illustrations in this book are true to life and are included with the permission of the persons involved. All other illustrations are composites of real situations, and any resemblance to people living or dead is coincidental.

Unless otherwise identified, all Scripture quotations in this publication are taken from the HOLY BIBLE: NEW INTERNATIONAL VERSION® (NIV®). Copyright © 1973, 1978, 1984 by International Bible Society. Used by permission of Zondervan Publishing House. All rights reserved. Other versions used include: the New American Standard Bible (NASB), © The Lockman Foundation 1960, 1962, 1963, 1968, 1971, 1972, 1973, 1975, 1977, 1995; *The Message: New Testament with Psalms and Proverbs* by Eugene H. Peterson, copyright © 1993, 1994, 1995, used by permission of NavPress Publishing Group; the Revised Standard Version Bible (RSV), copyright 1946, 1952, 1971, by the Division of Christian Education of the National Council of the Churches of Christ in the USA, used by permission, all rights reserved; The New Testament in Modern English (PH), J. B. Phillips Translator, © J. B. Phillips 1958, 1960, 1972, used by permission of Macmillan Publishing Company; the New Revised Standard Version (NRSV), copyright © 1989, by the Division of Christian Education of the National Council of the Churches of Christ in the USA, used by permission, all rights reserved; the Good News Bible Today's English Version (TEV), copyright © American Bible Society 1966, 1971, 1976; the New King James Version (NKJV), copyright © 1979, 1980, 1982, 1990, Thomas Nelson Inc., Publishers; the Holy Bible, New Living Translation, (NLT) copyright © 1996. Used by permission of Tyndale House Publishers, Inc., Wheaton, Illinois 60189. All rights reserved.

CIP DATA APPLIED FOR

FOR A FREE CATALOG OF NAVPRESS BOOKS & BIBLE STUDIES,
CALL 1-800-366-7788 (USA) OR 1-416-499-4615 (CANADA)

Printed in the United States of America

3 4 5 6 7 8 9 10 11 / 08 07 06 05 04

Contents

Acknowledgments

GOD HAS WORKED THROUGH MANY WONDERFUL PEOPLE TO SHAPE my life. Likewise, this book is the result of the influence of many people, and I am grateful to each person, named and unnamed.

David L. McKenna has been used by God to provide pivotal counsel in my life since 1968. His example, as president of Seattle Pacific University (as I sat as student body president on the Administrative Cabinet), is what started my career in Christian higher education. His counsel pointed me to my area of professional specialization, and his speaking and writings on Christian stewardship are what really "turned on the light" for my understanding about the biblical use of possessions.

Many friends around the country provided dialogue that enhanced the work, including Rick Bee, Joyce Brooks, Tim Ek, Brian Kluth, Dian Little, J. P. Moreland, Adam Morris, Paul Nelson, Sam Perkins, Scott Preissler, Walt Russell, Hudd Saffell, J. David Schmidt, and Dallas Willard, to name just a few.

The mechanics of research and producing this piece were assisted by several—Christa Benedetto, Michael Castro, Anne Creamer, Sarah Drayer, and Peter Freund. Also, those at NavPress played their significant parts: Greg Clouse, Cameron Crawford, Dean Galiano, Sue Geiman, David Hazard, Lauren Libby, Nanci McAlister, and Kent Wilson.

Martyn Smith was a capable partner in this project over several years, from concept development to final draft. He came alongside to assist with his competence and expertise as a researcher and writer.

My biggest encourager throughout life has been my mother, Diantha S. Willmer. More than anyone, she took a personal interest in this project over the years and offered suggestions of how to improve the effort, even with the passing of her husband of fifty-six years, in the middle of this undertaking.

I also thank God for Biola University president, Clyde Cook. Without his heartfelt love and support of me as a person, I would not be able to take on such projects "over and above" my full-time responsibility. Clyde is a wonderful model of a person who seeks to glorify God in all of his life, and who understands biblical stewardship and demonstrates it in his life.

Finally, I thank God for my wife of thirty years, Sharon, and for our adult children, Stephen Paul, Anna Kristell, and Jonathan Brian and his wife, Lindsay—all of whom God has used to shape my life.

Introduction

I place no value on anything I possess, except in relationship to the kingdom of God.

—DAVID LIVINGSTON

"OKAY CHRISTIANS, WE HAVE OUR FINAL EXAM TODAY," THE teacher proclaims as most of the students gasp in surprise. "Put away your books and paper. Keep only a pencil in hand. The time has come for you to account for how you have used the stuff in your life." The few who are prepared quickly and confidently put away their notes. The rest are shocked and angry, exclaiming, "What type of a teacher would do this after such a happy life?"

While few Christians seem to take seriously what they do with their possessions or stuff, Scripture makes it clear in Romans 14:12 and 2 Corinthians 5:10 that we are all to give an account of our lives to God at the end of our earthly existence. We will be asked questions about how we used our money and possessions, such as:

- Where did it all go?
- What did you spend it on?
- What was accomplished for eternity with all the things God entrusted to you here on earth?

Scripture further points out that God has entrusted us with His possessions as a test while on earth to determine the status of our soul in heaven (see Luke 16:1-9). As a result of this test, God is able to determine our spiritual maturity, and the character or condition of our soul for eternity. These are all serious issues of the Christian life.

My wife, Sharon, is a gifted teacher in higher education. She often talks about how differently students prepare for a final exam. Some study carefully over the duration of the term. Others never study until the night before the exam. Others act as though they have forgotten a test is even coming. Similarly, many Christians prefer not to consider how they will be judged at the end of life on earth.

It is a commonly held belief that the central focus of the Christian faith is to worship and walk with God in all areas of our lives. Lordship is the predominant topic of the sermons and Christian programs we listen to, the hymns and choruses we sing, the literature we read, and the small-group Bible studies we attend. From the Four Spiritual Laws to contemporary Christian music, putting God first in our lives through trust and commitment is a never-ending theme, "for there is within each of us a longing for love and intimacy that only He can fulfill."[1]

According to Scripture, one of the most important ways that we demonstrate the lordship of Christ in our lives is how we handle our possessions. By this God is able to measure our faithfulness on earth and determine our level of responsibility in heaven. How we handle our possessions is also a measure of our commitment to winning the world to Christ. Mature followers of Christ realize that how they handle their possessions is genuine evidence of godly spiritual formation in their lives. Scripture is clear that God entrusts us with possessions to teach us always to put Him first.

Despite this fact, most Christians struggle with the tension between their stuff and their spirituality. Philip Yancey speaks for many of us when he states, "I wish I did not have to think about money at all. But I must come to terms with the Bible's very strong statement about money!"[2]

Randy Alcorn hits the topic even harder: "Large segments of modern evangelicalism have succumbed to the heresy that this present life may be lived selfishly and disobediently without serious effects on the eternal state. Never have so many Christians believed that our monies and possessions are ours to do with as we please."[3] As Robert Wuthnow has found through his research, today's Christian finds little connection between faith and possessions: "There is a kind of mental or emotional gloss to contemporary religious teaching about money that prevents them from having much impact on how people actually live their lives."[4]

Our stuff and the spiritual development of our soul, however, are very important topics to God—so important that seventeen of the thirty-eight parables of Christ were about possessions. Possessions are mentioned 2,172 times in Scripture—three times more than love, seven times more than prayer, and eight times more than belief. About 15 percent of God's Word deals with possessions—treasures hidden in a field, pearls, talents, pounds, stables, and so on.[5] Obviously God understood that believers would find this a difficult area of their lives to turn over to Him.

Scripture repeats many times that if Christ is not first in the use of our money, He is not first in our lives. Our use of possessions demonstrates materially where we are spiritually. Is it possible that our checkbooks are a better reflection of our spiritual condition than the underlining in our Bibles? We are to be faithful managers and generous givers of what God has provided us.

The vision of stewardship in 1 Peter 4:10-11 (RSV) assumes that "good stewards of God's varied grace" are men and women who are grateful, merciful, and faithful, and called to covenant responsibility for all of creation. When we talk about stewardship, it is not just a dictionary definition. It is God's design for living as Christians in a nonChristian world through how we give of our time, talents, and money. Stewardship is God's way of raising people, not man's way of raising money.

The topic of faith and possessions is explosive—like walking in a snake pit or across a minefield. It is a "no-no" in many churches. We like to think that what is in our pocket, wallet, or purse is our own business—no one else's. The purpose of this book is to lovingly reaffirm the essential role that possessions play in forming the spiritual life "so that the nature of Christ becomes the natural expression of our souls, bodies, and spirits throughout our daily lives."[6] As a result, we will experience joy by being generous.

To accomplish this, chapter 1 traces three primary ways God links our possessions and our souls. Chapter 2 builds on this framework by developing the important issues of spiritual formation and soul development as tied to our possessions. Chapter 3 takes this discussion a step further by providing a device to measure the correlation between maturity of faith and use of possessions. Chapter 4 outlines ways in which we are able to be faithful stewards, and chapter 5 takes us back in time to see how early Christians such as John Wesley dealt with possessions. Chapter 6 points out that Christianity is currently failing to reverse the culture and historically demonstrates how this decline has taken place. Chapter 7 provides a practical framework for dealing with appeals by developing a philosophy of giving. What we should expect from our local church is the topic of chapter 8, while chapter 9 talks about the essential stewardship education that should take place in Christian families, colleges, and seminaries. Chapter 10 provides suggestions for Christians and their ministries on how to revitalize the roots of stewardship.

To return to the analogy at the beginning of the introduction, there are no makeup tests when it comes to handling our earthly stuff. The consequences to our eternal soul are being molded now. Every moment brings us closer to eternity and the outcome of whether our treasure was stored temporarily on earth or forever in heaven.

God's Map for Your Stuff and Your Soul

Jesus Christ said more about money than about any other single thing because, when it comes to a man's real nature, money is of first importance. Money is an exact index to a man's true character. All through Scripture there is an intimate correlation between the development of a man's character and how he handles his money.

—RICHARD HALVERSON

JOY SITS DOWN FOR A MOMENT AND WATCHES PART OF A TELEVISION program that her two sons watch every day after school. The action and plots are typical, but during the commercials her kids light up, pointing out particular toys they want. "Mommy, can I get that?" they plead at various times.

Joy and her husband both work outside the home to make ends meet, but she feels badly she can't get as many things as she would like for her children. Now it's toys, but in junior high it will be designer clothes, and then in high school a car. For a moment she feels resentful of the television that daily imports new desires into the minds of her boys. With a little more reflection she might have realized that the same phenomenon is true of her. As she and her husband watch a favorite television program, they too are bombarded with images of the "good life." And they dream about getting a better car or that new electronic gadget.

Joy and her husband are both Christians and faithful

members of their church; yet neither of them was taught how to handle the materialistic demands of culture in terms of their Christian faith. And in this they are like the majority of American Christians—possessions seem important and seldom have a link to their spiritual life. How can we live out Christian financial values in the midst of a consumer-oriented culture that teaches us always to want more? Is there a way to break free of these ingrained values? Does God's Word have anything to say about how a Christian is to handle his stuff in light of eternity? "As counter culture as it may seem, generosity is a virtue that's absolutely essential for a soul that wants to remain free and to grow in spiritual health. For the attitude we have toward our money and possessions reaches to the depth of us, to the very nature of our existence."[1]

Many of us feel that if we only had a little more money or possessions, somehow our life would get straightened out. We could pay off our bills and have money left over to give to God. We could get out of our present financial mess; we could live with some security for once, maybe feel at peace with God. But perhaps something is fundamentally faulty with this strategy of getting more and more. Our lives are filled with anxiety and dissatisfaction. And even when we get that pay raise, we don't give any more to God's work.

What we need is a different starting place, a different assumption for our lives. More is never going to be enough. My goal in writing this book is to help you find a sturdier foundation for dealing with your stuff—one that gets you off the treadmill of "more." It will happen when you rearrange the priorities of life to put God first.[2]

A TOOL, A TEST, AND A TRADEMARK
At the heart of ordering our relationship to God, our possessions, and our soul is understanding how God views this unique triangle. In the parable of the rich man in Luke 16, Jesus lays out three basic principles that would transform our lives if we only applied them. In summary, they are:

1. Our possessions are to be used as a *tool* to further God's kingdom here on earth;
2. They are given to us as a *test* to see how much responsibility we will be given in heaven;
3. They serve as a *trademark* to those around us that we are believers in the Lord Jesus Christ.[3]

Let's unpack the Luke passage a bit before looking at each of these principles in more detail.

In Luke 16:1-9, Jesus tells His disciples about a wealthy man who does not want to deal with his daily financial affairs, so he turns them over to a steward or investment manager. The manager has held this position for many years and is able to handle the job with little effort.

One day at the wealthy man's club, a friend comes to him and says, "Hey, it's probably none of my business, but yesterday I was at the market and I saw your manager making some bad transactions with your money." Again, later that day, while the wealthy man is eating dinner at the local café, he runs into another friend who says, "I know it's none of my business, but I saw your money manager, and you might want to check up on him. I think he's robbing you blind."

So the wealthy man investigates and, sure enough, the person he entrusted with all his wealth is mishandling it. Shaken from his complacency and red with anger, he calls in the financial manager and tells him, "I have the goods on you. You have twenty-four hours to bring all accounts up-to-date. Then hand over the record book; you're finished."

Realizing that he's about to be out of a job, the manager calls on his cunning. He says to himself, *I too am a highly respected person in this community. I am not going to dig ditches or beg.*

The manager's plan is to reverse his record (see verses 5-7). He sends a runner to summon everyone in the community who owes his boss money. When the first of the debtors arrives, he asks, "How much do you owe my boss?" "Eight hundred gallons of olive oil," the debtor replies. The manager counters, "Make it 400 and you owe no more." At this, the debtor looks at him in amazement and says, "What a bargain. Thank you so much. If there's ever anything I can do for you, let me know."

The manager asks a second debtor, "How much do you owe?" "One thousand bushels of wheat," is the response. The manager instructs, "Take your bill and cut it by 20 percent. You now owe eight hundred." The manager has done the debtor a favor, but the debtor does not know why. And this sequence repeats itself until every overdue account is addressed.

Within twenty-four hours, the manager had surrendered his keys. On the street he meets one of the debtors, who greets him warmly. The debtor asks, "How's it going?" The unemployed manager tells him a story of woe about the wealthy man coming on hard times and having to cut back his staff. The debtor, sympathetic to the man's plight, immediately takes him in. When the money manager meets other debtors and relates his twisted tale, they all feel sorry for him. Soon, he has a new circle of friends promising to provide him whatever he needs.

By this time, the disciples must surely be thinking, *What a crooked, evil man. I can't wait to see how Jesus will condemn this cheat.* However, Jesus surprises them by commending the dishonest manager because he had acted shrewdly. Then Jesus pulls out of the parable and makes this statement to all of us about possessions: "For the people of this world are more shrewd in dealing with their own kind than are the people of the light" (verse 8). He goes on to apply the parable, noting three principles that encompass and communicate how God views not just our money, but all of our stuff.

He begins by saying: "I tell you, use worldly wealth to gain friends for yourselves, so that when it is gone, you will be welcomed into eternal dwellings" (verse 9). He is referring back to the money manager who has used his limited time and opportunity to leverage for himself a secure future. As children of God's kingdom, we have only a short time to serve as managers in this world. Our lives could end at anytime. We should use the stuff we have as stewards to affect people for eternity.

POSSESSIONS AS A TOOL TO ADVANCE GOD'S KINGDOM

In essence Jesus explains, "You need to learn how to use your worldly possessions in such a way that when you enter heaven people will welcome you because of your resourcefulness." In short: You have limited time on this earth and limited opportunity with your possessions—use them wisely! God is instructing us to leverage our possessions so that when we enter our eternal home, we'll meet people who will say, "You don't know me, but do you remember when you gave to that Christian college? Do you remember when you gave to that church or Bible society? Do you remember when you provided that spare room in your house? Do you remember? (*Well, barely,* you think.) Well, know that I am in heaven because of the way you used your possessions on earth to further God's kingdom "

The question becomes: How are we leveraging our possessions—our car, our home, our clothes, our stocks, our time, our talents, our collections—to glorify God? Wise stewards will assess all of their possessions to determine if they are being used wisely as tools on God's behalf. The point is not about giving a percentage of income or giving away what we have, but what we are doing with what we have to advance God's kingdom.

POSSESSIONS: A TEST WITH ETERNAL CONSEQUENCES

The second principle is that our possessions are a four-part take-home test. This test is to:

1. determine who is master of our life
2. assess how much responsibility we will be given in heaven
3. determine how faithful we were in dispensing God's grace

4. see what honors we will receive at commencement into heaven.

As Randy Alcorn states, "God makes it apparent that it is His business to watch us with intense interest to see what we do with the money He has entrusted to us. We are being tested and what we do with our money will influence the course of eternity."[4] This final exam is a once-in-a-lifetime opportunity. There is no calling in sick, no retake, no rescheduling, no appeals to the department head or dean. When time is up, the game is over, and we have no excuse. How will you score on the final exam? (Chart 1-1 provides a practice test for you to see how prepared you are and what changes you may want to make in your life.)

Luke 16:10-12 states, "Whoever can be trusted with very little can also be trusted with much, and whoever is dishonest with very little will also be dishonest with much. So if you have not been trustworthy in handling worldly wealth, who will trust you with true riches? And if you have not been trustworthy with someone else's property, who will give you property of your own?" It is as easy to shortchange someone with a $10 bill as with $10,000. One does not need to mismanage a high-tech executive's fortune to prove oneself a poor steward; poor use of a weekly paycheck will serve to demonstrate the point as well. This is why our character is associated with our use of money.

God in heaven is looking down and saying, "For the span of your earthly life, I'm watching to see whose kingdom you're really committed to. And if I cannot trust you with worldly, temporary wealth, then why do you think when you enter my kingdom I will be able to trust you with true riches—riches that last forever? Besides it's not really your house, your car, your dining-room table, your 401k. If you died today, it would remain here and you would not. It is not yours; you are simply a steward."

Part one of the test, then, is to determine our lord and master—God or stuff. We cannot serve both God and money (Luke 16:13). Each moment of our lives we are making choices to leverage and use the possessions we have to either benefit our lives on earth or to invest in heavenly stock. This is why our checkbook and credit card statements are a better reflection of our soul's health than any Christian service we could render. This life on earth is the preface, not the book. There is no cheating on this test, for God knows our attitudes and our actions better than we know them ourselves.

The second part of the take-home test is to demonstrate how much responsibility we are worthy of assuming in heaven. Do you remember in grade-school gym class when the teacher selected someone to be captain? The captain had earned the right, through responsible behavior, to select who would be on his or her team and what positions they would play. The captain's leadership would by and large determine the team's success. Similarly, here on earth we are demonstrating to God what we are able to be responsible for in heaven.[5]

What if at the judgment seat of Christ we are shown to have been irresponsible with the money entrusted to us? And what if our assignments in the world to come are meager because of our ineffective management here? This brings our possessions into focus as a Christian trust, not merely a medium of exchange to serve our own private ends. Our possessions are something that God gives us; then He steps back and allows us to work. As a result of the decisions we make on earth, God will assign us proportional responsibilities in heaven.

The third part of the take-home exam is to assess how well we have shown ourselves dispensers of God's grace. This facet of the test arises from a passage like 1 Peter 4:10, which instructs us to be "good stewards of God's varied grace" (RSV). Or, as other translations suggest, we are called to be "good managers" (TEV) or "faithful dispensers of the magnificently varied grace of God" (PH).

The thinking behind being dispensers of God's grace is threefold: (1) God creates abundance; therefore, we sense ourselves as overwhelmingly gifted; (2) God is gracious;

Chart 1-1

Take-Home Practice Test to Final Exam

God has entrusted us as stewards of His possessions while we are on earth, as a multipart test (Luke 16). After assessing how we use our possessions, God is able to determine our spiritual maturity, character, and how much responsibility we will be given in heaven for eternity. Your answers below will help you predetermine how prepared you are for the final exam at the end of your earthly life.

1. Who is master of your life—God or your stuff? (Luke 16:13) After reviewing your credit card statements, your checkbook, and looking over your possessions, take a sheet of paper and list specific examples that demonstrate that God's eternal kingdom and your soul are your highest priority (Luke 16:1-9).

2. Make a list of all the possible people who will welcome you in heaven and thank you that they are there because of how you used your stuff to accomplish God's work of winning others to Christ. This list will be two parts: one is the direct result of what you did, and the other is the results of a person or ministry who was doing God's work because of your support—for example, a missionary who leads people to Christ.

therefore, we celebrate God's grace; and (3) God is generous; therefore we are sent into the world to be imitators of God.[6] Our giving is reciprocating God's grace. Acts 2:44-45 and 4:32-37 show how the early Christians shared all they owned and even liquidated their possessions to give to others as they had need. "Much grace was upon them" and "There were no needy persons among them" because they gave sacrificially. How common is that today? Are we imitators of God in dispensing His grace to those around us?

Part four of the test is God's assessment of what honors or crowns we will earn in heaven. Scripture points out that we will receive rewards in eternity according to what we do on earth and that the degree of rewards will vary (Proverbs 24:11-12; Matthew 19:27-30; Luke 14:12-14). It may come as a surprise to many Christians, but the Bible indicates our reward levels in heaven will differ (1 Corinthians 3:12-15)—not all of us will have the same position of authority (Luke 19:17,19,26). We will not all have treasure in heaven (Matthew 6:19-21), and unfortunately, not all Christians will hear the Master say, "Well done, good and faithful servant!" (25:23).

Not only can we fail to receive rewards, we can forfeit rewards already in our account. So we are to guard our own crowns (Revelation 3:11) because we can be disqualified from earning them (1 Corinthians 9:27), lose them (3:15), or have them taken away (Matthew 25:28-29). John warns us, "Watch out that you do not lose what you have worked for, but that you may be rewarded fully" (2 John 8).

In summary, God will reward you according to how you pass the test of what you do with your money and possessions, and it will affect your experience in heaven. The choice is yours: pleasures here or rewards later.

TRADEMARK OF WHO MADE US

We live in a culture of brand loyalty and market shares. Businesses spend huge amounts of money to persuade us what to drink, drive, and wear. Each of these products has a trademark well-known to all of us. In fact, companies will pay millions of dollars for mere seconds to

Take-Home Practice Test to Final Exam (cont'd)

3. Cite five ways that you are leveraging the use of your possessions on earth to glorify God in heaven.
4. List ten examples from the past year that demonstrate you are using your generosity to grow God's kingdom.
5. How much responsibility will you be given in heaven (Luke 16:1-9)? If you were sitting in a room with God today and He asked you to justify how much responsibility you should have in heaven as a result of being a faithful steward of your stuff on earth, what would you say?
6. Write a one page essay, citing specific examples of how you are an imitator of God's grace through how you use your possessions (1 Peter 4:10).
7. List specific examples throughout your life of what you have done to earn crowns in heaven as a "good and faithful servant," by how you have used your stuff on earth.
8. Make three lists—one each for neighbors, friends, and coworkers—that demonstrate specific evidence (by how you use or don't acquire stuff) that your trademark is that of a Christian (Luke 16:13).

promote their trademark during prime-time television.

As your neighbors, friends, or colleagues look at you, what brand or trademark do they see? Are you "of this world" in how you use the possessions entrusted to you or are your values reflective of someone created by God and striving to serve Him?

Luke 16:13 brings us back to this truth: "No servant can serve two masters. Either he will hate the one and love the other, or he will be devoted to the one and despise the other. You cannot serve both God and Money." We either serve God or we worship our things.

Try taking inventory of all you have. Ask yourself, "Am I using this room for God or myself?" How about that car or timeshare? The second home, spare room, or the abundance of food in the refrigerator? This is serious business in God's sight, and if we take these truths to heart, it is sobering to consider how we must reorder our lives so that our neighbors, business associates, and friends will know we are committed Christians by how we use our earthly possessions.

IT IS POSSIBLE!

If this all seems overwhelming and impossible, don't despair. While it is not easy, it is possible to turn your life toward God in the use of your possessions. The following is the story of one man and his family who found a way out of the maze of conflicting demands from the world and silence from the church to the promised land of financial freedom.

Brian and Sandy Kluth are similar in many ways to millions of baby boomers: they live in suburbia, own a home, and have three children. Both are college graduates; they are committed Christians, attend church regularly, have two cars, and live on a middle-class income. What makes them different from millions of other such couples is that they have gained control of their financial life. They have made a conscious choice to put God first in all their financial decisions. In recent years they have given away between 20 and 40 percent of their income each year. They are now coming to a place where they will set a certain income as being enough for their needs, and anything over and above that amount will be given for causes that build God's kingdom.

Just as important as the fact that they are generous givers is the fact that their possessions do not possess them, and they have been transformed in this spiritual discipline. They realize the link between their faith in God, their possessions, and their souls. They understand that possessions are a tool of God, a trademark of their faith, and that their choices are a heavenly test.

No one, of course, is born a giver. Just as sharing does not come naturally to a young child, so giving money is not an automatic act when that child grows up. Brian Kluth did not grow up as a Christian. And he had imbibed the belief of our culture that somehow happiness could be had if only he had a little more money or a few more things. These values led Brian to steal from friends and employers (and even family). Every time he took something it seemed that the goal had skipped one step further away; satisfaction lay always just beyond his grasp. Before he could give, he had to find a way to break free of the controlling power of money. He needed a new foundation for his life, a new organizing principle for his financial choices.

When he became a Christian at age twenty-one, he realized that stealing was wrong, and he stopped such overtly sinful behavior. But he still didn't know how to find true happiness. He approached life in much the same way, only now he charged those items on his credit card instead of stealing them. And he found himself accumulating an unmanageable debt. Brian began to realize that although he was a Christian, he was not living his life according to Christian principles. As he began to be exposed to more teaching about giving, he concluded that he needed to get serious about this area of his life, and fundamentally to turn around his ideas as to where happiness and satisfaction lay. At that point he felt God calling him to commit at least 10 percent of his income to spiritual things.

This basic commitment to be honest with God in his personal finances led to some basic lifestyle choices as well. Brian's eye-catching Chrysler Cordoba began to look a little different to him. Realistically this gas-guzzling car was simply too expensive for him at this stage in his life, his mid twenties. He sold it for cash and bought a less expensive vehicle. It wasn't quite riding in style, but it did more accurately reflect his financial means. And this was just one of many such choices that his newfound commitment to God brought about.[7]

These choices, which inevitably come when we get real about our financial life, are the tools by which God shapes our material and spiritual lives. As we learn to reorder our lives and make service to God our highest priority, we make financial choices that begin to reflect that new internal value system. As Brian found out when he made the choice to sell his sports car and get a more modest vehicle, these choices are not necessarily easy; but by making them we slowly begin to bring our lives into conformity with Christ, which is the ultimate goal of the Christian life.

Brian Kluth's story is proof for other Christians that a way exists out of financial frustration. Of course, there is no one way to escape frustration. Americans are accustomed to the "dieting" mentality, which looks for ten easy steps to lose frustrations. The answer to frustration is not to copy the steps that another person has taken. At the root of most financial troubles are spiritual battles that must be dealt with before external actions can be changed.

Like Brian, many Christians mistakenly believe that more money will bring financial security and freedom from anxiety. This internal attitude controls our financial choices. Once and for all, that inner stranglehold must be loosened by Scripture's clear teaching. As that inner orientation is changed, God's values become the primary motivator, and we can then take concrete steps to bring life into line.

One point in Brian's story that could easily go unnoticed is that the change in his financial and spiritual life did not come the day he became a Christian. Several years transpired between his initial acceptance of the gospel and his understanding of how the gospel would change his financial habits. The Christian life begins at the moment of faith, but it does not end there. It involves a steady march of spiritual growth and change. A person's eternal destination is settled at the moment of faith, but building a life pleasing to God takes the rest of his or her life. Although the effort is unavoidable, at the end of this pursuit the Christian finds true happiness and satisfaction (qualities that had been elusive before).

While American Christianity has emphasized getting people saved, it has not spent nearly as much time and resources teaching disciples how to lead the Christian life. And one of the most crucial areas where teaching is needed is that of the Christian's use of money and possessions. Jesus said, "You can't worship God and Money both" (Matthew 6:24, MSG). God is not indifferent to our daily financial choices, but is interested in transforming all of our lives.[8]

As with other disciplines of the faith, the disciplined use of possessions is not meant as a burden. In the end, the Christian will find that this discipline of being generous leads to a joy and satisfaction, if only he or she will let God reorder this intimate part of life.

CHAPTER TWO

Spiritual Growth and Your Stuff

What good is it for a man to gain the whole world, yet forfeit his soul?

—MARK 8:36

AT THE CORE OF SPIRITUAL GROWTH IS THE REALIZATION THAT ALL believers have a choice as to which kingdom they will follow, the temporary kingdom here on earth or the eternal kingdom where our soul will dwell forever with God. It is a choice we must make deliberately or it will be made for us.

On paper this would seem like a no-brainer—something believers would not give a second thought. For example, James 4:14 suggests that our life on this earth is "a mist that appears for a little while and then vanishes." Likewise, in Isaiah 40:6-8, God says life on earth is so brief that we are like grass that grows up in the morning and wilts in the afternoon. Why would anyone in his right mind even consider putting all his investment into this fleeting life?

Scripture depicts the Christian who is not investing in eternity as shortsighted or blind. *Unwise* is too weak a word. As stupid as the fool in Luke 12 is more like it. Our central business here on earth is to prepare for the next life, not for a comfortable retirement.

Jim Elliot, the missionary martyred decades ago by the Auca Indians in Ecuador, echoed this same theme when he said, "He is no fool who gives away what he cannot keep to gain what he cannot lose." Two centuries earlier, John Wesley said, "I value all things only by the price they shall gain in eternity."

"The one who dies with the most toys wins" was a popular bumper sticker a few years ago. While it is cute in some ways, it is also a sad portrayal of our prevailing cultural value. It reinforces the commonly held belief that life ends at the time of our bodily death, that there is no eternal soul that outlasts life on this earth, and that the accumulation of possessions is therefore the only goal that makes sense for this life. While Christians generally deny that they think of life in this way, their actions and accumulation of the same "toys" would suggest otherwise.

Randy Alcorn verifies this attitude when he states:

> Our perspective on and handling of money is a litmus test of our true character. It is an index of our spiritual life. Our stewardship of money tells a deep and consequential story. It forms our biography. In a sense, how we relate to money and possessions is the story of our lives.[1]

Dedicated Christians throughout history have understood the wisdom of laying up treasure in heaven instead of on earth, but why do many Christians adopt the opposite attitude and lay up material possessions on earth? One answer lies in money's unique ability to mimic God in an attempt to meet practically every need we have. In his book *A Christian View of Money*, Mark Vincent gives seven reasons why money is godlike: (1) it outlives you; (2) its circle of influence is greater; (3) it is mysterious; (4) it lives among the things we are tempted to worship; (5) it mimics everything promised in the New Jerusalem; (6) it is an instrument you wield; (7) and everything can be economized.[2]

The more wealth replaces God in our lives, the less we have need for Him. C. S. Lewis puts it this way: "Prosperity knits a man to the world. He feels that he is 'finding his place in it,' while really it is finding its place in him."[3]

The Lure of Materialism

The idea that human life can be fulfilled through material things has been with us since Creation. A. W. Tozer suggests, "There is within the human heart a tough, fibrous root of fallen life whose nature is to possess, always to possess. It covets things with a deep and fierce passion."[4] The contemporary "me" society we live in, with its abundance of toys and opportunities for wealth, makes this a very difficult part of our lives.

It was no different in ancient times. From the lures of Egypt and Canaan for the Israelites to the New Testament struggles of individuals as diverse as Judas and Ananias and Sapphira, the major competitor for God's kingdom has been the pursuit of money and possessions. Money worship is a violation of the first and most fundamental of the Ten Commandments: putting something before God Himself. From the Bible's viewpoint, materialism is actually greed or idolatry (Colossians 3:5). Scripture also suggests that greed is the source of almost every destructive force, including war (James 4:1-3). The pursuit of things is considered the root of our social evils and apostasy (1 Timothy 6:10). Over and over the Bible warns believers against taking the false path.

Of course the extreme reaction to materialism is asceticism, a lifestyle of depriving oneself of all but the bare essentials. There is little biblical evidence to support such an extreme position, because the appropriate use of money, wealth, and possessions as outlined there is threefold: (1) to care for one's own family and thus prevent them from becoming a burden to others (1 Timothy 5:8; 1 Thessalonians 4:11-12; 2 Thessalonians 3:6-15); (2) to help those in need—especially the church (Proverbs 19:17; Romans 15:25-27; Galatians 6:7-10); and (3) to encourage and support the work of the gospel both at home and around the world (1 Corinthians 16:1-3; Philippians 4:14-19; 1 Timothy 5:17-18).

Clearly there is no need for the Christian to disavow money and possessions. As Craig Blomberg asserts in his book *Neither Poverty Nor Riches: A Biblical Theology of Material Possessions,*[5] Scripture calls for a balanced view of how we use our things. God gives us lots of latitude to make choices about how many cars, houses, pairs of shoes, and on and on. The point here is not to draw a hard and fast line, but to shift our mind to the crucial question: "Is my life things-centered or God-centered?"

If we desire our lives to be God-centered, then we need to be aware of the strong influence of culture around us, and start to turn our lives toward building His eternal kingdom. The smart thing in God's eyes is to be a caring, loving, and sharing person. But how do we get off the well-beaten track of our materialistic culture and onto the less-traveled trail?

THE PATH TO SPIRITUAL FORMATION

A starting point is to realize that we have an eternal soul connected to our material possessions. This is not the thinking of our culture. As Oprah Winfrey, probably the best spokesperson for our wider culture, says, a person's soul is simply "the best part of who you are."[6] She leaves it at that. Many Christians today are willing to leave it at that also. This common opinion only illustrates how far we are removed from historical truth. It reflects a world-view that sees human beings as having finite and limited value, rather than infinite worth.

The soul is a very complicated entity with an intricate internal structure. It is not the role of this book to explain the soul in detail. However, it is important to acknowledge that the soul does exist and that it "is a substantial, unified reality that informs its body. The soul is to the body what God is to space—it is fully 'present' at each point within the body. Further the soul and body relate to each other in a cause–effect way."[7]

As Christians we have become familiar with the fact that invisible realities exist. We believe that God Himself doesn't "live in temples made by human hands" (Acts 7:48, NLT). But both believers and nonbelievers live in, and interact with, a world full of immaterial things, including numbers, ideas, concepts, moral values, relations, properties, universals, and sets.[8] This understanding of immateriality has a bearing not only on our practical lives but on our understanding of who we are as persons. If we are by nature human beings with eternal and infinite value, as well as eternally existing immaterial persons at the core, then how we handle our possessions is of immense importance both in how it can affect other people of infinite worth as well as how it can mold and shape our own eternal souls.

In the gospel accounts, Jesus connects the human soul to material possessions. Jesus had begun to disclose to His disciples the true nature of His mission on earth: that He would soon undergo great suffering, even physical death, but that He would be raised on the third day. Incredulous, Peter takes Jesus aside and rebukes Him for false teaching. Perhaps his audacious action comes out of fear of personal material loss or out of concern for the well-being of his teacher. Whatever the reason, it is clear from Jesus' stinging counter-rebuke (see Matthew 16:23) that Peter had his mind on earthly rather than spiritual things. Jesus then begins to instruct His disciples on the meaning behind self-denial and implicitly on the effectual power possessions can have upon our souls. Literally, He says, "For what will be benefited a man if the whole world he might gain, but his soul he might lose" (Matthew 16:26).[9] Jesus establishes a connection between material things and spiritual things. It is evident from this passage that eternal life is not only about the "heart," and the material realm affects more than simply other material objects such as our physical bodies. The statement, "Where your treasure is, there your heart will be also" (Matthew 6:21), is double-sided. Just as our literal treasures affect our heart, so the state of our heart, or soul, affects how we handle our material treasures.

Once you realize that you have a soul and that there is a clear connection between earthly possessions and the eternal soul, the next step is to think about spiritual growth or changing your soul.

IT IS POSSIBLE TO CHANGE YOUR SOUL

In C. S. Lewis's book *The Great Divorce,* Lewis paints a picture of what it might be like after death in our disembodied state prior to the final resurrection. Lewis portrays self-absorbed people as literally weak and insubstantial, so insubstantial that they, even in this kind of pseudo-paradise, are injured by blades of grass as knives, and by drops of water as bullets. In this hypothetical intermediate world, it is the person's choices and beliefs during life that shape the final state of his soul after death, and either make that soul weak or strong in the afterlife. In other words, people shape their lives in such a way to make it either possible or impossible for them to enjoy heaven.

Long before C. S. Lewis, Aristotle wrote concerning character:

> Character arises as we behave in certain ways, as we engage in certain activities. . . . Thus . . . states of character arise out of like activities. This is why the activities that we exhibit must be of a certain kind. It is because the states of character correspond to the differences between these. It makes no small difference then whether we form habits of one kind or another from our very youth. It makes a very great difference or rather all the difference.[10]

If our character is necessarily a reflection of the state of our invisible soul, then, on the flip side, any change in character will result in the reforming and reshaping of our souls. The ascetics of the medieval ages understood this well, though they erred in taking material possessions to be inherently evil rather than inherently good (this being the proper biblical view: "and God saw that it was good," Genesis 1:4,10,12,18,21,25).

Common sense tells us there is more at stake than temporal harm when persons are influenced by their peers to engage in bad actions, for bad actions often lead to bad habits, and in turn our character and even our eternal soul are affected.

THE PATH TO CHANGING YOUR SOUL

Okay, given that it is possible to change our soul, how do we go about this process of changing our soul *for the better?* What causes internal transformation? If our body and soul are connected, it would make sense that the actions we perform repeatedly have an effect on our souls. This idea is not new. God had this principle in mind when He gave Moses the Ten Commandments (Deuteronomy 5). God was not trying to be authoritarian, but He was genuinely concerned about the lives of His people. He knew that guiding their outward actions would help them to maintain healthy souls. God's laws—such as the Ten Commandments—are not arbitrary, but reflect the fact that God created human beings to function in certain ways. When we do not follow God's laws, we become spiritually and relationally distant from Him, and we are unfulfilled. When we follow His commands, we function in the way God created us to function. As a result, we experience His closeness and a wholeness and satisfaction we can never obtain otherwise.

Today we know the conscious practice of inner transformation through outward actions as "spiritual discipline." Over time, Christians have come to recognize certain "spiritual disciplines." These are specific kinds of actions that in Christian experience have tended to build spiritual maturity, activities done not for their own sake, but "to make us capable of receiving more of [God's] life and power"[11] and to move people into a deeper spiritual relationship with Him. These disciplines include on the one hand such positive acts as prayer, worship, study of God's Word, and service to others; and on the other hand acts that require a sacrifice of some kind, such as fasting, chastity, and solitude. Historically these have been avenues by which Christians have deepened their walk with God. As Richard Foster succinctly writes, the disciplines "put us where

[God] can work within us and transform us. . . . They are God's means of grace. . . . God has ordained the Disciplines of the spiritual life as the means by which we place ourselves where he can bless us."[12] Other disciplines have included silence, frugality, secrecy, sacrifice, celebration, service, fellowship, confession, and submission.

Each of the spiritual disciplines has as its aim the reordering of a certain area of our lives. By allowing God to use spiritual discipline and by exercising general, everyday discipline, we are shaped and changed into the godly pattern of life. One of these disciplines has to do with one's use of money. For the writers of Scripture, this financial discipline is one of the most important aspects of the whole Christian life. Unfortunately, it is frequently forgotten. For the writers of Scripture, the spiritual life is intimately tied up with how a person views possessions. A person's financial life is a reflection of his spiritual life. If God is first in a Christian's use of possessions, then He has opportunity to shape the spiritual life dramatically.

This practice of forming one's soul through the exercising of outward discipline so that one's life is more and more integrated and dominated by God's spiritual kingdom is what is commonly known as spiritual formation. In Galatians 4:19, Paul writes, "My little children, for whom I am again in the pains of childbirth until Christ is formed in you." Paul uses the Greek word *morpho* ("to form"). A New Testament scholar writes: "Growth of Christ in believers is compared to development in the womb. This growth is an ongoing process, both open and secret, and both a gift and a task, with maturity as the goal."[13] In other words, it leads to spiritual transformation.

If God requires such activities of us based on His knowledge of what is best for us, why do we not see biblical teaching on our use of possessions in the same light? In fact, generosity is actually mentioned in the Bible, right alongside love, joy, faithfulness, and peace. It is clearly considered an activity that is to be a constant part of the Christian life—just as love, joy, and faithfulness are. Given the hundreds of references to money and wealth in the Bible, it is strange that the lifelong habit of generosity with our material possessions is not stressed as much as love, joy, peace, and faithfulness.

Having seen the relation between a spiritual discipline such as giving and the spiritual vitality of our soul, we can see that possessions are powerful instruments—not only in what they accomplish in the world, but in what they can accomplish in our souls. Transforming our attitude about God and possessions is paramount in our decision to pursue the kingdom of heaven. Jesus expressed this when He said, "For where your treasure is, there your heart will be also" (Matthew 6:21).

GOD MADE US TO GIVE

This biblical use of our possessions involves responsible personal use of our God-given wealth, as well as generous giving to others and to God. This exercise of giving might better be referred to as "spiritual giving." We take part in "spiritual giving" not out of our love for our neighbor primarily—though this is certainly important. Neither is "spiritual giving" done in order to gain some return on our investment, either materially or because we expect God's blessings. How many sermons have we heard where we are encouraged to give because of what we can expect God to give back in return? I recently heard a sermon where the pastor's primary motivation for giving was based on God's commands as declared in Deuteronomy 28:12 (NRSV): "The LORD will open for you his rich storehouse, the heavens, to give the rain of your land in its season and to bless all your undertakings."

No one denies that God delights in blessing us when we follow Him. However, this material emphasis misses the deeper meaning of giving. We "spiritually give" because, as a lifelong spiritual discipline, it has the power to *form us* and with God's help *transform us*. To say it another way: In developing our skill at giving, we unify our entire self and come into a more genuine relationship with God. By giving more of ourselves (time, money, talents), we are also giving more of ourselves over to God, shaping our own souls.

Jesus understood the power of riches because of our fallen state. A New Testament scholar writes on Jesus' teachings:

> In Matthew Jesus abandons the traditional view of riches in favor of one that is wholly theocentric and eschatological. Neither wealth nor poverty is significant in itself (cf. 27:57). The delight in riches (13:22) and the difficulty of salvation for the rich (19:22ff) simply typify the human situation in which nothing is gained even by winning the world if the soul is lost (6:25ff), and the anxiety of pagan life stands in marked contrast to seeking righteousness and the kingdom (6:25ff).[14]

Even before Moses, Abraham paid tithes to Melchizedek (Genesis 14:20; Hebrews 7:6), and even before Abraham, Cain and Abel gave of what they owned to God (Genesis 4:4). In Leviticus 27:30, everything is proclaimed to be the Lord's and we must give back from what He has given to us. Worship, in its biblical sense, is not just about music. Giving from our money and possessions is a major part of worship—recognizing and proclaiming God as the true owner of all material things.

Just think of how such an understanding of giving would affect our churches and our sermons. Instead of giving to help the church, or to get material rewards only, what if we truly believed that we are to give because God created us to give, that it protects us from spiritual poverty, and that our souls are actually changed and improved in the process?

LIFESTYLE CHOICES
The bottom line of the trail less traveled in regard to spiritual growth and your stuff is that it will most likely affect

your lifestyle. Your focus will shift from building up your earthly kingdom to building up the kingdom where your eternal soul will dwell. The goal is to maximize resources for kingdom work. Here is a formula:

1. Make all you can. (God desires to bless you.)
2. Live as inexpensively as possible (with contentment).
3. Provide maximum resources to God's kingdom work.

What this formula implies is that everyone should strive to be as prosperous as God blesses. The key distinction is what proportion are you able to use for eternal kingdom work. If God chooses to prosper your work, it is not so you can live luxuriously, but so that you can give and leverage more for eternal causes. This generosity shows where your heart is—that your hope is in God and not in yourself or your money.

In his book *Desiring God,* John Piper suggests that we should think in terms of a "wartime" lifestyle rather than a merely "simple" lifestyle. Simplicity can be very inwardly directed, and may benefit no one else. A wartime lifestyle implies that there is a great and worthy cause for which to spend and be spent (2 Corinthians 12:15).[15] Piper goes on to state "we should be content with the simple necessities of life because we could invest the extra we make for what really counts."[16]

The generation that was living during World War II knows that all lifestyle choices revolved around saving resources so they could be used for the war effort. My parents frequently talked about not taking trips to save gasoline, using as little electricity as possible, or saving tin cans for use in the war. Similarly, our current generation needs to be called to a higher "eternal kingdom" wartime vision of our lifestyle. Only as we are willing to deal with these issues of lifestyle can we truly take the spiritual trail less traveled.

Scattered throughout the book of Proverbs are wise counsels on money and possessions. The values found there form an essential backdrop to the Christian life. Proverbs 3:5-6 (NRSV) contains the well-known passage, "Trust in the LORD with all your heart, and do not rely on your own insight. In all your ways acknowledge him, and he will make straight your paths." In the verses immediately following these we find a proverb dealing specifically with the use of wealth: "Honor the LORD with your substance and with the first fruits of all your produce" (verse 9, NRSV). Clearly part of "acknowledging him in all your ways" is using money and possessions in a godly manner—which means giving from one's abundance to God. Since God is the One who gives all abundance, and we are stewards of that abundance, it is right to acknowledge that gift by giving back to God.

Numerous proverbs indicate wealth is a result of following wisdom: "The hand of the diligent makes rich" (Proverbs 10:4, NRSV) or "prosperity rewards the righteous" (Proverbs 13:21, NRSV). Living by God's principles really does bring material increase. Many Christians have been surprised to find that when they get with God's program, their financial life begins to make sense. The kind of commonsense financial advice in Proverbs is still important for contemporary Christians to put into practice.

Money and possessions may be gifts from God, but at some point comfort turns into luxury, and at that point it becomes liable to God's judgment. There is a tremendous amount of freedom in the Christian life, with a few specific lifestyle boundaries prescribed in Scripture. We do not look to the Bible to learn how big our television should be or how expensive our new car can be. But in making choices such as what kind of car to drive, how much to spend on a house, or where to take a vacation, it is imperative for the Christian to keep in mind the message of the prophets; lifestyle choices are not a matter of indifference, but something for which we are eternally responsible.

THE PEARL OF GREAT PRICE
The Bible is not a book of rules. This disappoints some people who are looking for exact guidelines by which to

live, while others are glad since it means they can justify living any way they want. Both of these groups have missed the heart of the matter, which is Christ. The Christian is someone who has found riches that boggle the imagination. It is for this reason that Jesus in His well-known parables compares the kingdom of heaven to a "pearl of great price" or a "treasure hidden in a field." The richness of this treasure is so great that the persons who find it sell all they have in order to acquire it. They realize that in comparison to this perfection all they own can be discarded.

This is an illustration of the Christian and the use of possessions. For the man or woman who has found the spiritual life available through Christ, all that is offered by the "good life" of this world now is seen for what it truly is: vanity, a chasing after the wind. A person's attitude toward money and possessions undergoes a fundamental change. Things are now tools for the pursuit of this greatest good, not thrown away or neglected, but used strategically to gain this pearl.

Not that this attitude adjustment is always without a struggle. More than one person since the rich young ruler has turned away from this biblical mandate, feeling that it is just too much to sacrifice. But for anyone who has actually seen the pearl, for anyone who has actually tasted the riches offered in Christ, to anyone who has contemplated the surpassing excellence of the treasures to be found in heaven, no sacrifice is too great. To gain the pearl is all that matters to the merchant. And to know Christ and to live a life of obedience to Him is what truly matters to the fully committed believer.

CHAPTER THREE

Marks of a Mature Steward

If you love Christ and the work of His kingdom more than anything else, your giving will show that. If you are truly submitted to the lordship of Christ, if you are willing to obey Him completely in every area of your life, your giving will reveal it.

—DONALD S. WHITNEY[1]

IN DAILY CONVERSATION WE REGULARLY ACKNOWLEDGE LEVELS OF spiritual maturity. For example, we call young Christians "babies in Christ," implying that they have only recently made a confession of faith and are being nursed on milk as a child until they can take in solid food like an adult. A primary contention of this book is that a believer's attitude toward money, possessions, and giving is one of the more accurate measures of this spiritual maturity. Randy Alcorn, citing the New Testament examples of both Zaccheus and the rich young ruler, agrees: "There is a powerful relationship between a person's true spiritual condition and his attitude and actions concerning money and possessions."[2]

This chapter is designed to elaborate on this point by outlining the stages of faith developed by James W. Fowler in his book of the same name. Fowler's work provides a theoretical framework or benchmarks that define stages of spiritual maturity, which we all fit into at some level. I'll summarize Fowler's faith stages, then follow with what I believe are corresponding stages of giving (see

Chart 3-1). The intent is not to become legalistic or inflict guilt, but to produce a helpful guideline to measure your own spiritual maturity by how you handle your possessions and to give you a goal to work toward.

Fowler's Stages of Faith

Using the well-established theoretical models of Piaget, Selman, and Kohlberg, James Fowler mapped out six stages of faith. Besides drawing from these existing developmental models, he conducted interviews with people from a variety of religious backgrounds. M. Scott Peck calls this work "the classic book on the subject of faith development."[3] As Fowler explains in the introduction, "Theories can be exciting and powerful, giving us names for our experiences and ways to understand and express what we have lived."[4] His work helps each of us answer such questions as:

- For what goals or organizations are you pouring out your life?
- To whom or what are you committed in life? In death?
- What activities get your best time?
- With whom do you share your most sacred hopes?

In other words, as we have already glimpsed in previous chapters, these stages of faith answer the all-important question: Who is master of your life? At what level of maturity is your faith? Developed along lines of human growth, here are Fowler's Stages of Faith, with a brief description of each stage, its dangers, and how to progress to the succeeding stage. Keep in mind that while these stages imply age-group development, physical age is not necessarily a factor. As we all know, an adult can easily still be in a childlike faith stage.

Stage 1: Intuitive-Projective Faith

As Fowler explains, "Our first 'reasoning' involves sensorimotor knowing."[5] Typical of an infant's or toddler's development, this stage involves imitation of examples. Behavior is frequently composed of the moods, actions, and stories present in the people surrounding the individual.

The danger at this stage is that faith-related fears can lead to rigidity or authoritarianism, in which taboos and faulty moral or doctrinal expectations are reinforced.

At the heart of transitioning to the next stage is the quest to know how things are and to clarify the bases of distinctions between what is real and what only seems to be.

Stage 2: Mythical-Literal Faith

This stage of faith is like the school child before adolescence—he adopts the beliefs and behaviors of those around him. He views God as anthropomorphic, and stories become the primary method of giving unity and value to his experience. He takes role models literally and believes the world ought to be a place of reciprocal fairness ("an eye for an eye").

The danger of this stage is that literalness and the desire for reciprocity can lead to an overcontrolling outlook, perfectionistic tendency, or righteousness by works. It can also lead to a keen sense of being bad due to mistreatment or neglect by others.

The transition to the next stage is like the process of moving into physical adolescence. It is uneven because the person enjoys the comfort of the literal view of life, but is torn to define an individual faith experience.

Stage 3: Synthetic-Conventional Faith

This stage is like going into puberty; it brings a revolution in physical and emotional life as a new personality emerges and a few trusted others start to be the primary shapers of it. The person hungers for a God who knows, accepts, and confirms him. Faith gives structure and meaning to all his spheres of interest, including family, peers, school, and work. Faith helps define identity and relationships tend to shape faith. At this stage, faith ideas have not melded together into a cohesive "philosophy of life" and conformity to others is fairly common.

The danger of this stage is that the internalization of other people's faith and judgments can cause a person to lose his or her own autonomous decision making and behavior. Also, failures in interpersonal relationships can lead one to question the reality of God as completely dependable and unconditional. This is a stage where many adults remain throughout their lives.

Stage 4: Individualative-Reflective Faith

Like someone in young adulthood, at this stage the person takes more serious responsibility for his own faith and feels more self-certainty in his beliefs. At the same time, tensions of faith include: (1) individuality versus being defined by others; (2) subjectivity versus objectivity and critical examinations; (3) self-fulfillment versus service to others; and (4) relativity versus absolutes.

The dangers at this stage are generally twofold: the person can become overly confident in his own ability to think critically or he can become overly receptive to the faith definitions of others.

The breakdown of this faith stage that creates a readiness to transition to the next may include: serious clashes or contradictions between valued authority sources, changes by sanctioned leaders, or changes in policies or practices previously deemed sacred.

Stage 5: Conjunctive Faith

Evidence of this stage is the ability to see many sides of an issue simultaneously and to examine and scrutinize inner inconsistencies and prejudices. Faith is like looking at a field of flowers through a microscope and wide-angle lens simultaneously. A person's true commitment to justice and the carefully defined faith boundaries are not as "black and white" as in the previous stage. He also has a genuine interest in reaching out to develop the faith of others. While certainly the faith of a mature adult, it is possible to move to an even wiser place.

Stage 6: Universalizing Faith

This last and supposedly ultimate step of faith maturity results when the person has little regard for self-preservation and lives out absolute love and justice as much as possible. He is unshackled by manmade social, political, and religious rules. Life is a matter of spending and being spent for the good of others and building God's kingdom. This is truly a God-centered stage of faith maturity that many seek but few achieve.

At the core of these six stages is the tension between self-centeredness and God-centeredness. So too when we examine the measurement of our faith through how we use our possessions.

MEASURING OUR SOUL MATURITY AND POSSESSIONS USE

Thomas Schmidt refers to Christian discipleship as a journey: "We begin at different points and we move at different rates . . . but the biblical message is clear enough about [the] destination."[6]

Again, in looking at these stages (chart 3-1), they are intended to be a guide. Many of us adapt several stages at once and can move from one to the other at different times in our lives. The easy analogy is that the stages correspond to our age: stage 1—toddlerhood, stage 3—adolescence, and so on to mature adulthood. However, while that is a convenient way to conceptualize these stages developmentally, in actuality, stages transcend one's life span from birth to death. Growth is not automatic. It is very possible, and even probable, that a person becomes stuck and remains in a stage for his entire life. In fact, many people never progress beyond stage 2 or 3. It is also possible for someone to become a Christian in midlife or later and to progress very quickly, to even seemingly skip stages as he matures in his faith and use of possessions. Since our use of possessions is an accurate barometer of our faith, chart 3-1 helps explain this relationship.[7]

Chart 3-1

Correlation of Soul Maturity and Use of Possessions

Stages	Faith Characteristics	Evidence in Use of Possessions
Stage 1: Imitator	Like a child, is marked by imagination and influenced by stories and examples of others.	Is able to mimic the examples of others in giving when shown or instructed.
Stage 2: Modeler	Takes beliefs and moral rules literally. Perception of God is largely formed by friends.	Gives sporadically when given an example to follow.
Stage 3: Conformer	Faith becomes a basis for love, acceptance, and identity; involves most aspects of life; and is shaped mainly by relationships. Faith does not yet form a cohesive "philosophy of life."	Gives because it is the thing to do. Likes recognition, tax benefits, and other personal gain from giving.
Stage 4: Individual	Begins to "own" one's faith. Faith is less defined by others as one becomes able to personally examine and question one's beliefs.	Starts to give in proportion to what God has given. Danger of becoming prideful regarding giving or giving for the wrong motives. Wonders why others do not give more.
Stage 5: Generous Giver	Grasps the main ideas of an individualized faith as well as individual practices. Becomes interested in developing the faith of others.	Recognizes that all one owns is from God. Begins to give of one's own initiative, rather than out of obligation or routine. Derives joy from giving.

Stages	Faith Characteristics	Evidence in Use of Possessions
Stage 6: Mature Steward	Little regard for self. Focuses on God and then on others. Free from manmade rules.	Recognizes the role of a faithful steward of God's possessions. More concerned with treasures in heaven than on earth. Content with daily provision.

Stage 1: Imitator

The easiest analogy of an imitator is the young child who gets a dollar allowance, and before Sunday school class is told by his parents, "Here's a dime to put in the offering plate." While the child does not realize the purpose for giving, he obeys because he is instructed to do so (and he may see his parents doing the same thing at the worship service). Another example is the adult who puts a dollar or two into the offering plate because others are reaching for their wallet or checkbook.

These beginning points in faith and use of possessions can best be described as imitating or mimicking. At this stage, people understand little about the faith and give only if someone else suggests it as a good idea. This stage is characterized by the physical act of doing.

One man that I interviewed puts 10 percent of all his business's profits into a foundation each year and then gives the funds to Christian causes. When I asked him how he started this practice, he responded, "When I became a Christian in my late forties, I just assumed by watching others that when you accepted Christ, you start to give." He has now internalized his reasons for giving and matured in his faith. His use of possessions, however, began as a mimicking process, with little internal conviction as to why.

In stage 1, the giving behavior is learned from other believers, which can be a problem in a church where money and possessions are seldom discussed. Teaching at this first stage ideally takes place with small pieces of digestible information, consistent with the analogy of feeding a small child.

It is possible to get stuck at this level if a person remains completely dependent on a spiritual mentor—someone he imitates—to tell him what to do. Many, however, move to the second stage.

Stage 2: Modeler
In this stage, a person sees principles as "black and white" in a world of reciprocal fairness. If he is aware of the concept of a tithe, he will generally try to make a radical change in his giving pattern. Seldom, however, does this pattern last. Stage 2 behavior is similar to the eight- to eleven-year-old child for whom behavior vacillates.

A modeler frequently puts something in the offering plate solely because he feels it is the right thing to do. And like children at this age, he is subject to strong swings in his giving. One day he fully supports God's kingdom work, the next his personal needs take priority. This is followed by pangs of guilt and a swing back to deep devotion. The pendulum goes back and forth during this "literal faith" stage because the internal value structures are not present to stabilize lifestyle and behavior.

An example of a modeler who is not giving is a twenty-three-year-old college graduate in her first year as a nurse. Wanting lots of stuff right away, she uses the convenience of a credit card to buy a dog, more furniture, a top-of-the line espresso machine, and a mountain bike. While she has learned about giving from her Christian parents, she is not making ends meet and blames her lack of income. So giving is not a priority for her and seldom happens. When the offering plate is passed, she puts in a token dollar. Whether she will ever progress to the next stage is unknown.

In this modeler stage, perfectionism can come into play: "Look, I am doing this the correct way. What's wrong with the rest of the believers? Why don't they give at a more generous level?" This "If I can do it, why can't you?" attitude is often short-lived.

Stage 3: Conformer

In stage 3, a person begins to develop a little more internal depth to his giving. He sees how giving affects others around him, how it can benefit him personally, and even recognizes more fully his moral and biblical obligation to give. But at this stage, as in the first two, he is still often focused on the horizontal aspect of giving. In other words, his primary reason for giving is to fulfill practical needs and satisfy his sense of personal obligation.

We can think of the giver at this stage as the conformer. The conformer gives for convenience's sake, might be motivated by tax benefits, and will readily give small amounts for purposes of recognition. Taking on debt may not be a problem for the conformer. This person's giving is probably in the 2 percent range of income. Generally he gives from what is left over and not off the top.

The conformer, or self-centered giver, generally compartmentalizes faith and finances. That is, he sees little connection between belief in a personal God and how he handles his possessions. Many Christians, I assert, are in this category. Most stay stuck here throughout their earthly life and never really become liberated by understanding the vital link between their eternal soul and earthly possessions. Convenience and relationships tend to shape their behavior rather than internalized convictions of faith.

Stage 4: Individual

Stages 1-3 involve formation of one's understanding of giving, but at stage 4, one's view of giving begins to undergo transformation. Not only does such a person continue to mature in his giving by giving more freely and more often, and by experiencing the joy that comes when putting the needs of others above one's own, but also, partly as a consequence of this, he begins to see giving as something central to his human existence. He begins to realize that spiritual growth occurs as he sees the spiritual element in the proper use of his possessions.

Likened to a young adult, this person is stepping out

with more confidence in his faith and giving, even though he is not always successful. Giving is less defined by others and becomes more of a personal concern. Lifestyle changes are possible for this giver.

A good example of a person at this point in his life is Dave Adrian, who, after graduating from George Fox University in Oregon, started working for a very modest salary, barely enough to make ends meet. After a year and a half he found that he was giving to God very sporadically. Instead of giving his first fruits to God he gave out of whatever was left at the end of the month. Not only was he struggling with faithfulness in giving, but he was saving less than ever. About this time Dave did some soul searching and the Lord impressed on his heart that He would provide for Dave's needs as he honored God with his first fruits (Proverbs 3:9). In response, Dave made a commitment to give 10 percent of his income to God, put 10 percent in savings, and live off the 80 percent remaining. He did this for three months and to his amazement found that he never depleted his checking account. He couldn't figure it out except to conclude that this was God's economics. Dave realized that God was meeting his needs as he gave first to God. As Dave's income has increased with age and he has become a father, he continues the practice of always writing the first checks of the month to his church and the other ministries he supports.[8]

Dave's story is a good illustration of how we can successfully step into stage 4 as we rely upon God's provision. At the time we receive our paycheck we may not see how we can possibly give to God and still meet all our financial needs. Though this may be the case, God is calling us to give to Him first and trust Him to provide the rest. No matter the method we employ, our effort to give to God first will deepen our faith and give us an increased desire to serve His eternal kingdom.

At this individualization stage, the vertical issues of soul development really start to become internalized and giving becomes a lifestyle of faith.

Stage 5: Generous

As Gary Thomas espouses, "Fulfillment comes in being vessels of the generous heart of God by giving of our wealth and substance."[9] God made us to give ourselves away to get back our life. At stage 5, a person begins to further detach himself from earthly possessions and material security, and to depend more on God. He also experiences continued vertical soul growth, even to the extent that people see him as a role model in this area, and he begins to desire to teach others about the significance of giving. Giving becomes much more integrated into his spiritual life, rather than just his daily life. In other words, he begins to realize that giving fulfills a deep human need he was created for; and as he gives, his dependence upon material possessions weakens.

A good example of a generous steward is David Beckman. While still in seminary he learned the importance of giving, and those teachings were foundational to his tenure of more than thirty years as the president of a Christian college. He strove to promote quiet giving, all the while taking the leadership position in fund-raising at the school. His efforts were rewarded because he developed deep relationships with donors—becoming their friend, pastor, and mentor.

During lean years at the college, David often denied raises and opted not to receive his salary for months at a time in lieu of the faculty getting paid. He loaned thousands of dollars to the school at no interest to keep it solvent. He personally underwrote the expenses of several students who could not afford to eat or buy books, or who needed additional funds to stay in school. Often the Beckmans put their personal assets on the line—a risky but necessary option when the future of a school was at stake.

When asked why he and his wife chose to live such a frugal life to be able to give to others, they recalled that during their seminary years their cupboards were often bare except for a bag of rice or a can of broth. When things seemed quite hopeless, acquaintances would stop in with bags of groceries, asking that the gifts be returned at some later date by giving to someone equally in need.

Giving for the Beckmans has evolved over the years. Never ones to think their giving should be limited to their tithe, they began giving in ways that brought them great joy.[10] First, they have learned that often it is in not taking that one finds the greatest joys. Acts such as refusing a salary and not accepting payment for conducting weddings or funerals do not show up on any kind of donor list, but are an important part of their giving life. Second, they have found that giving to individuals in need may not reap a tax benefit but proves the most rewarding. Third, while it may be wise to gain the tax benefits of giving, it often cuts out the joy. The Beckmans' giving certainly is internalized and makes them generous stewards.

Stage 6: Mature Steward

As a mature steward, a person develops a firm conviction that God truly owns everything, just as it is written in Leviticus 27:30 (NRSV): "All tithes from the land, whether the seed from the ground or the fruit from the tree, are the LORD's; they are holy to the LORD." A mature steward gives not knowing where money will come from and gives more so that others can experience spiritual and material benefits.

A mature steward's vertical understanding or "spiritual giving" matures as well. He views giving as something very intricately bound up with material concerns. He starts to see how powerful God is when he depends on Him instead of worldly things. His character and soul are actively being transformed by his new understanding and use of his possessions, and he becomes a more spiritual human being. Just as God "gave his one and only Son" (John 3:16), he is actively imitating God in giving more of his possessions. In effect he is surrendering some of his dominion, and experiencing a freshness of life as a result. At this stage a person can say along with Paul, "For I have learned to be content with whatever I have. I know what it is to have little, and I know what it is to have plenty.

In any and all circumstances I have learned the secret of being well-fed and of going hungry, of having plenty and of being in need. I can do all things through him who strengthens me" (Philippians 4:11-13, NRSV).

John Wesley is a good example of a mature steward. John Wesley was a very influential teacher on the topic of giving.[11] To many he is known as a great preacher, but few are aware that he also made a substantial amount of money from preaching and the sale of his books, making him one of the wealthiest men in all of England At a time when thirty pounds a year was enough for a single man to live comfortably, Wesley took in as much as 1,400 pounds! With such a high income he had the perfect opportunity to live in luxury, but Wesley refused the temptation and lived a life of incredible generosity.

When Wesley was at Oxford, an event happened that changed his perspective on giving forever. After putting some pictures on his walls that he had recently purchased, a cumbermaid came to his door in need of some help to keep her warm. Unable to help her because he had purchased the pictures, Wesley quickly realized that God was not pleased with the way he was spending his money. He asked himself the probing question, "Will thy Master say, 'Well done, good and faithful steward'? Thou hast adorned thy walls with money which might have screened this poor creature from the cold! O justice! O mercy!—Are not these pictures the blood of this poor maid?"[12]

Wesley's lifestyle was so countercultural that the English Tax Commissioners were completely confused by it. They insisted that a man of his stature must have silver plates in his possession that he was not paying taxes on. To which Wesley replied: "I have two silver spoons at London and two at Bristol. This is all the plate I have at present, and I shall not buy any more while so many [a]round me want bread." When Wesley died in 1791 at age 87 the only money he left behind was that found in his pockets and dresser. Chapter 5 provides more on Wesley as a mature steward.

As the six stages demonstrate, there is an intimate

relationship between our eternal soul and how we use our earthly stuff. Chart 3-2 provides a graphic illustration of the choice we make between God's eternal kingdom and earth's finite kingdom, as explained in chapter 2. The chart depicts how the stage 1 (Imitator) individual shows low spiritual maturity while the stage 6 (Mature Steward) individual values highly and acts upon the use of his possessions, with an eye on God's eternal kingdom.

These six stages, then, provide a paradigm for you to assess where you are in the vital link between how you use your earthly possessions and the effect these actions will have on your eternal soul. We all make choices each day as to the trail we will follow. The next chapter outlines the steps to become a faithful steward.

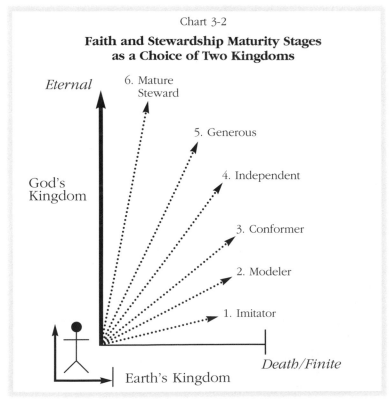

Chart 3-2

Faith and Stewardship Maturity Stages as a Choice of Two Kingdoms

Eternal

6. Mature Steward

5. Generous

4. Independent

God's Kingdom

3. Conformer

2. Modeler

1. Imitator

Death/Finite

Earth's Kingdom

CHAPTER FOUR

How Then Shall You Become a Faithful Steward?

Stewardship is nothing less than a complete lifestyle, a total accountability and responsibility before God. Stewardship is what we do after we say we believe, that is, after we give our love, loyalty, and trust to God, from whom each and every aspect of our lives comes as a gift.

—RONALD VALLET[1]

PAUL HUBBLE SPENT MOST OF HIS CAREER AS AN INDUSTRIAL ENGINEER for the Boeing Company in Seattle. Born in 1913, he went through the Depression and knew what it meant to have little money. Christ entered his life when he was thirty-seven, well after he had married and had a family. During a social time at my mother's church in Seattle, I asked Paul out of the blue: "What is the relationship between your possessions and your soul?" From most people such a question would get at best a blank stare and perhaps an end to the conversation. But Paul responded without hesitation: "How I give is a measure of my faith in God. It is part of maturing in Christ. It is a form of worship that is part of my spiritual life. It is a reflection of my whole spiritual condition." And while finishing his coffee he continued explaining how God wants Christians to be faithful stewards of the resources entrusted to them: "We should give a tenth—and that not of the net but of the gross. God will judge us by the fruits of our lives, and how we use our possessions is a more accurate reflection of the maturity and condition of our soul than the underlining in our Bible."[2]

Needless to say, I was impressed; it is not often one hears the biblical view of stewardship elucidated so clearly. Unknowingly Paul has hit upon many of the themes of this book. He understands that his attitude toward money is a test of his faith in God; he sees that giving is a tool for deepening his own spiritual life; and he recognizes that giving becomes a trademark that will identify him as a genuine Christian. In the midst of a culture that works hard to compartmentalize faith, fewer Christians and Christian organizations today understand this vital link between faith and giving. Yet as R. Scott Rodin reminds us, "The concept of the godly steward is not an add-on to the 'proper' teaching on the life of the Christian, but instead it lies at its very heart. To be a Christian is to be a steward in the kingdom of the triune God of Grace."[3]

The bulk of this chapter provides ten biblical principles of becoming a faithful steward, after which we will look at what the Bible has to say about tithing.

I. DECLARE WHO IS LORD OF YOUR LIFE

The Bible's teaching on money and possessions is never better stated than Jesus' words in the Sermon on the Mount. Speaking to the crowds from the mountain, He says: "No one can serve two masters; for a slave will either hate the one and love the other, or be devoted to the one and despise the other. You cannot serve God and wealth" (Matthew 6:24, NRSV). Jesus put the choice in stark terms: complete commitment to discipleship, or service to the world and its ephemeral pleasures. No comfortable, middle position exists. Which side of this divide you fall on is the first and essential question for becoming a faithful steward. This is the test that Jesus lays out for His followers and, while for contemporary Christians it may seem like a surprise test, it shouldn't be—it's in the syllabus! Nothing is hidden about the importance of complete commitment of all money and possessions to God.

Okay, now that we've resolved that all your money and possessions are God's, what next?

2. Understand What a Faithful Steward Is

Jesus and the New Testament writers offer a stewardship approach as guidance for the Christian financial life. The clearest instance of this worldview is found in Jesus' Parable of the Talents (Matthew 25:14-30). In the story, a rich man who was going on a journey called together his servants and entrusted property to them. He gave one of the servants five talents, another two talents, and to a third he gave one talent. While this may not sound like much, each talent was equal to fifteen years of wages for a common laborer, so a substantial amount of money was involved. The servant entrusted with five talents used that capital for trading, and made five more talents with the investment. The servant entrusted with two talents did the same thing, and made two more talents. But the third servant went and dug a hole in the ground to store the talent entrusted to him, and thus made no profit from it.

When the master returned home and settled accounts, the servant with five talents and the servant with two talents both could demonstrate they had profited handsomely, doubling the money entrusted to them. The master rewarded each one accordingly: "Well done, good and faithful servant! You have been faithful with a few things; I will put you in charge of many things" (verse 21). But when the last servant came forward and had nothing to show for his talent, the master became angry. Instead of burying the talent, why not invest the money with bankers, so at least interest would have accrued? His response to this last servant was harsh: "Take the talent from him, and give it to the one who has the ten talents. . . . And throw that worthless servant outside, into the darkness, where there will be weeping and gnashing of teeth" (verses 28,30).

By this parable Jesus again shows Himself exceedingly interested in the financial choices of His followers. The master who goes away on the long trip is analogous to God, who also leaves His people with certain gifts. Like the servants, we are entrusted with personal, financial, and social gifts to be used—invested—in a manner that furthers God's kingdom. At the end of time God will return to His household and demand that each of us account for the way in which we used those gifts.

The parable not so subtly instructs us that if we are smart, we will behave as stewards and treat our possessions as a tool to help grow God's kingdom and our soul. It is necessary to carefully consider how our possessions can best reap a profit in the spiritual world. We are instructed by Jesus to be savvy investors, with our eyes fixed on long-term spiritual gains.

3. Count Your Blessings—You Have More Than You Realize

Once you have declared God as Master of your possessions, you may be discouraged because of the big task before you. Johnson Oatman, Jr. wrote these words to the hymn "Count Your Blessings," taken from Psalm 40:5:

> When you look at others with their lands and gold,
> Things that Christ has promised you His wealth
>   untold:
> Count your many blessings money cannot buy
> Your reward in Heaven, nor your home on high
> Count your blessings, name them one by one.
> Count your blessings, see what God has done.[4]

This inventory taking helps you put in perspective how to be thankful and sensitive to God's blessings in your life. Here are some blessings that you may not have considered as important, but which have great value:

Family: How has God blessed you with your family? Parents, brothers and sisters, a husband or wife, children?

Friends: Who surrounds your life? Family friends, personal friends, friends from church, other acquaintances?

Health: What are the good things about your health for which you can thank the Lord?

Food: Most of us, far from having to worry about starvation, have at our fingertips more than we need.

Home: Think of the place you call home. Thank Him for the comfort of your house—heat, running water, toilets, electricity, and a bed.

Clothes: Thank God for the clothes that He has so graciously provided you.

Work: Thank God for the opportunity He has given you to work and provide for yourself and your family.

Money: Consider not just your main income, but also the unexpected gifts that come your way—the possible appreciation in your house and the profits you have seen in your investments.

Faith: Do you have hope beyond the physical boundaries of this life? Thank God for hope in this present life and in the life to come.

Through this exercise, you are able to see clearly the creative ways that God has blessed your life. You will be surprised as you recall the friend who took you out to lunch, the hand that a neighbor gave in difficult yard work, and even the less-than-ideal crop of tomatoes in the garden. With this mind-set you'll begin to give, not out of compulsion or because you've been instructed in Scripture to do so, but out of a grateful response to what God has first done. Giving is no longer a chore, but a joyful response.

4. Give to God First—Just Do it!

At the end of each month Gail places a pile of bills on her kitchen table and prepares to pay them. She writes out check after check, paying her mortgage, car payment, car insurance, utilities, and so on. When the messy pile has finally metamorphosed into a neat stack of envelopes, she sits there, back slouched and head resting in her hands. Once again the bills and expenses have swallowed everything. Her goal each month is to have something left over to give to her church and to a couple of Christian charities. Those gifts will be put off for yet another month. What seems strangest to Gail is that according to all her figuring it should not be like this. She is making more at her job than ever before, yet somehow the bills grow at the same pace as her earnings—if not faster.

Why do so many of us experience this same result? While there are undoubtedly as many answers to this question as there are people, the main reason we have so little to give is because we have not learned to give to God first. We may have good intentions to be generous in our giving, but the money is gone before we have a chance to give it.

A college student came to me not long ago, struggling with one of her greatest frustrations. With her demanding course load she was no longer able to find time for Bible reading and prayer. The time she did manage to spend with God was sporadic and left her discontented. It was not long before we got down to the heart of the matter. Before she took any time for God, she tried to complete all her other daily demands. Once she made this self-realization, she decided to reverse her strategy. Remarkably, she found that if she set aside inviolable time to spend with God, she was still able to finish her school demands as well.

The principle this student learned is one that we all must learn. We must give to God from the top—not from the leftovers. When first we pay the bills, buy groceries, and cover all the incidentals that eternally come up, we no longer have money left to give to God. Our giving to God comes to resemble the time Gail spent with God—sporadic and ineffective.

5. GIVE TO GOD SYSTEMATICALLY

Some of you are surely thinking, I desire to give to God first, but I constantly find that the level of my desire does not correspond to the level of my giving. This is not uncommon. Once we establish the importance of giving to God first, we need to set up practical ways to ensure that we are faithful in our resolve (1 Corinthians 16:2).

Often we have good intentions, but are tripped up by a lack of discipline in our method of giving. Financial planner Ron Blue discusses this lack of planning:

> We plan for retirement or for starting a business or for funding our children's education, but few of us have a plan for giving. There will always be unlimited ways to use limited resources, and— unless we plan ahead—we will only be able to give the leftovers, if anything. Even an increase in our salaries won't make any difference. Needs always expand to meet income.[5]

We can order our lives to set aside a portion of our money for God, a portion for our savings, and a portion for spending. In fact, some people open additional bank accounts in order to separate money to be given to God from household expenses. Others have established automatic withdrawals from their checking account to ensure that a portion of their income goes directly, and faithfully, to God's work. Christians in India set aside the first of their rice and eggs in order to give to their pastor's family.

6. Give According to Your Means

In 2 Corinthians 8:8-12 (NRSV), Paul tries to inspire the Corinthian believers into giving generously, as the Macedonians had already done. He writes these words:

> I do not say this as a command, but I am testing the genuineness of your love against the earnestness of others. For you know the generous act of our Lord Jesus Christ, that though he was rich, yet for your sakes he became poor, so that by his poverty you might become rich. And in this matter I am giving my advice: it is appropriate for you who began last year not only to do something but even to desire to do something—now finish doing it, so that your eagerness may be

matched by completing it according to your
means. For if the eagerness is there, the gift is
acceptable according to what one has — not
according to what one does not have.

Perhaps the first thing to notice in this passage is that
Paul does not resort to asking for a tithe. This would be
the perfect time for him to say, "By the way, now that you
are all Christians, you need to start tithing like it says in
the Old Testament." He recognizes that giving is not something that can be prescribed by rules. What he does is to
assume some common points of Christian experience. If
the Corinthians' lives have truly changed, and they are
devoted to following the Lord Jesus Christ, then they will
have an eagerness to give their money and possessions for
the good of the church. Paul points out that he has wit-
nessed this inner change in their lives, and now asks that
their giving follow that inner change.

Upon hearing Paul's words, the responsibility for
each member of the Corinthian church would be to consider, given his financial situation, how much he could
send to the impoverished churches for which Paul was
raising money. As the Corinthians made this decision
they were to keep in mind the example of Jesus Christ
who "though he was rich, yet for your sakes he became
poor" (verse 9, NRSV).

How do Paul's instructions to the Corinthian church in
the first century A.D. apply to believers nearly two millen-
nia later? The idea of giving "according to your means" is
a timeless principle. Christians are called to give in conformity with their level of prosperity. The single mother
who is barely making ends meet should clearly not be giving the same percentage as a professional pulling in a six-
figure salary. Yet we are all called to honestly examine our
financial means and give what we can to God, remembering the sacrifice of His Son, who for the sake of our salvation gave infinitely more than any of us could contemplate
giving.

7. Give Cheerfully

The phrase "God loves a cheerful giver" has become a cliché for many Christians. Somehow we are supposed to smile as we drop those hard-earned dollars into the offering plate. Fortunately, the apostle Paul's words in 2 Corinthians 9:6-8 (NRSV) can become more than just a cliché.

> The point is this: the one who sows sparingly will also reap sparingly, and the one who sows bountifully will also reap bountifully. Each of you must give as you have made up your mind, not reluctantly or under compulsion, for God loves a cheerful giver. And God is able to provide you with every blessing in abundance, so that by always having enough of everything, you may share abundantly in every good work.

Paul is not looking for people who are compelled to give by rules and manipulation, but from their own internal convictions. If treasure in heaven is the true goal of life, then one can be cheerful while giving up treasures on earth—treasures that are bound to disappear in any case. Many Christians are unable to be cheerful when they give because they have never known this inner change.

This passage also brings up the topic of rewards for giving. Paul writes, "The one who sows bountifully will also reap bountifully" (verse 6, NRSV). In our day of "health and wealth" teaching, this verse is given all sorts of spins. You may have heard it explained as if God makes some kind of reciprocal promise: you give one dollar, God will give you two. But this approach vulgarizes the promise. It would be as if Paul promised that if the Corinthians give their earthly treasures, God would give them more earthly treasures. Such a message goes against the entire teaching of the New Testament. Giving is a tool, not for obtaining greater wealth on earth, but for obtaining the spiritual life that God desires for us.

8. Give Regularly

In Paul's first letter to the Corinthians, he also mentions giving. There he writes:

> Now concerning the collection for the saints: you should follow the directions I gave to the churches of Galatia. On the first day of every week, each of you is to put aside and save whatever extra you earn, so that collections need not be taken when I come (1 Corinthians 16:1-2, NRSV).

This passage is yet another chance when Paul could have easily mentioned the tithe. If Paul expected a flat 10 percent from Christians, he could have told them that at the start of each week they are to put aside 10 percent of their income. But instead of such specific instructions, Paul states: "whatever extra you earn."

Although Paul insists on freedom as to the amount given, he recommends that Christians find a way to systematically give. He wants the Corinthians to give regularly while he is away so that when he returns to the church he will not have to take any special collections. His recommended method for the Corinthian believers is to set aside money on the first day of each week, which was the day when Christians met together.

The timeless principle here is not to be found in the exact instructions given by Paul, but rather in the exhortation to be regular in giving to God's work. If your paycheck comes twice a month, then perhaps that is the interval at which giving should occur. Once a month works fine as well. But if you wait until a need arises, then chances are the money will be gone or committed elsewhere. It makes sense that giving not be a series of traumas, but planned and consistent.

Regular and consistent giving is also a way that God uses to make giving a trademark of the Christian life. Recently as I approached the front of our church on a Sunday evening, a man on his bicycle rode up to me and handed me an envelope. "Would you please make sure this gets in the offering plate?" he asked. Regular giving was so important to him that he made a special trip to church to see that it happened.

9. GIVE TO GOD GENEROUSLY AND QUIETLY

This phrase may conjure up visions of guilt-laden sermons on giving. But to get its true meaning, listen to this modernized account of a well-known gospel story.

> The room outside the sanctuary of the church bustled as one service got out and another was about to begin. Some milled around to talk while others rushed into the sanctuary to find a seat before the service began. In the anteroom there was a small box for money given to the Lord. As people departed or entered, some would toss money into the box. One woman who had recently lost her husband came and put a small offering into the box. Jesus spoke of this woman: "This poor widow has put more into the treasury than all the others. They all gave out of their wealth; but she, out of her poverty, put in every-thing—all she had to live on." (Mark 12:41-44)

This story captures the heart that Christ desires us to have. This woman's small gift cost her a great deal, certainly more than the much larger gifts left in the box by wealthy church members. She gave out of her poverty, trusting that God would provide. She did not give in order to be seen by others or for the small effect the gift would have on the ministry of her church, but rather out of gratitude to God. This woman understood that giving was a tool used by God to shape her into the spiritual person He wanted her to be.

In the eyes of God, such a gift is more generous than those given out of a sense of duty. This generosity is not a guilt-induced urge to give more and more, but a heart response within reach of every Christian.

10. GIVE REGARDLESS OF YOUR CIRCUMSTANCES

Where we put our treasure is an undeniable indicator of where our heart is. This speaks volumes, though not positively, for the state of the church. In fact, the problem is so significant that a majority of churchgoers have thousands and thousands of dollars in debt racked up. According to Crown Financial Ministries, the average family spends $400 more than it earns each year and 23 percent of the average person's net income goes toward paying existing debt (not including the mortgage on the home).[6] Of course, debt is not only a major problem in the church, but among the American public in general. *Time* magazine notes that nearly 14 percent of our disposable income goes to repaying loans—the highest percentage since 1986.[7] Assuming that the average Christian carries a debt roughly equal to the average American, Christians pay about 11 percent more toward their debts than to Christian work. Larry Burkett states that typical callers to his radio program carry a balance of $7,000-$10,000 on their credit cards, owe an average of $6,000 in educational loans, have $20,000 in car loans, and owe an average of $120,000 on the mortgage of their homes.[8]

This matter of debt competes with our love and devotion to Christ. If we do not find a way to control our spending habits we will continue to find giving a burdensome and difficult matter.[9] The best way to break out of this pattern is to give our first fruits to God, and live off what remains. Until we learn to give to God regardless of our circumstances we will never be fully committed to Christ and His kingdom.

Having established ten key principles of giving, we turn now to the question that confronts every Christian who has decided to take seriously the biblical practice of giving: tithing.

WHAT ABOUT TITHING?

Possibly one of the most feared words in the Christian vocabulary is *tithing*. For many people this word conjures up memories of stern sermons from the pastor on the necessity of giving 10 percent of all one's income to the church. Many Christians also associate tithing with legalism because it is not directly taught in the New Testament and seems at odds with the gospel's message of freedom. But it is an important concept to come to terms with, since it is the most practical way to attempt to bring our financial life into line with the teachings of Scripture—whether we follow it or not.

The basis for the tithe—which means the "tenth"—is found in the Old Testament. Deuteronomy 14:22-23 (NRSV) says, "Set apart a tithe of all the yield of your seed that is brought in yearly from the field . . . so that you may learn to fear the LORD your God always." How did this look in practice? Check 2 Chronicles 31 where King Hezekiah restores true worship to Israel, and commands that the people give from their resources as part of that worship. "As soon as the word spread, the people of Israel gave in abundance the first fruits of grain, wine, oil, honey, and of all the produce of the field; and they brought in abundantly the tithe of everything" (verse 5, NRSV). Out of all they produced, the Israelites owed God a tenth.

What this system of giving means to Christians has been debated since the early church, and that debate has not abated today. As stated earlier, many argue that no mention is made of the tithe in the New Testament. On the other side, those who tithe argue that tithing as a law was never specifically rescinded, and so is in force for the Christian today and even is much more than a tenth.

Perhaps there is a middle ground in this debate. It should be no surprise that the New Testament does not mention the tithe. The whole point of Jesus' teachings is that discipleship demands commitment of all of life. The rich young ruler was asked to sell everything he had and give it to the poor. Imagine if he had countered, "How about if I tithe every month?" Somehow, it seems doubtful that Jesus would have been satisfied. The stakes are higher in the New Testament. It is about complete commitment, offering ourselves as living sacrifices. The tithe has been rescinded because it no longer summarizes what God expects of those who follow Him. And if Christians think that all God wants is 10 percent, and that the rest is their own to do with as they please, they are sorely mistaken.

So does this mean that the idea of tithing should be thrown out, that the concept no longer be taught in our churches? While tithing may not be the total of what God commands, it has certainly served as a useful benchmark for giving—one which many Christians have been blessed for following. Christians need goals and examples, and the tithe has proved to be a practical mark that Christians can strive for in their giving. Randy Alcorn provides several practical arguments for the tithe: It is "clear, consistent, and transferable—that is, it can be easily taught to others. . . . Tithing can also be a significant factor in spiritual growth."[10]

Jesus demands all, but every Christian knows well enough how the cares of the world are apt to squeeze away all one's resources. A tithe serves for many as a first step to learning how to give all to God. So the tithe is useful, but should not be taken as the summation of the Christian's financial duty to God. Like the Law in general, it is the "schoolmaster" that leads us to the fuller demands of the gospel.

CHAPTER FIVE

Lessons from Earlier Christians

Those who cannot remember the past are condemned to repeat it.

—GEORGE SANTAYANA

ON JULY 10, 1666, ANNE BRADSTREET EXPERIENCED THE DEVASTATING loss of her house and possessions by fire. In a poem copied onto a piece of loose paper, she reflected on this experience:

In silent night when rest I took
For sorrow near I did not look
I waken'd was with thund'ring noise
And piteous shrieks of dreadful voice.
That fearful sound of "fire!" and "fire!"[1]

One can imagine this Puritan woman, living on the edge of the wilderness, wakened by the raging flames and cries of warning from those outside her family's cozy wooden house. Although she and her family escaped with their lives, the incident gave her an opportunity to reflect on the nature of material possessions and earthly life.

"It was His own, it was not mine," she tells herself, sounding one of the basic themes of stewardship: our material possessions are gifts from God, and held in trust. They are not "ours" to do with as we wish, or to cling to unthinkingly. Second, her gaze is inevitably drawn to greater spiritual treasures:

Then straight I 'gin my heart to chide:
And did thy wealth on earth abide,
Didst fix thy hope on mouldering dust,
The arm of flesh didst make thy trust?
Raise up thy thoughts above the sky
That dunghill mists away may fly.

Those possessions lost in the flames had become
anchors that chained her soul to the earth and took all her
attention. Spiritual triumph comes when the eyes are liberated from their downward cast and lifted to heaven.

There have been times in Christian history when the
connection between the spiritual life and the material life
was clearly drawn, when various teachers were clear
about the sacrifices inherent in Christian commitment and
the spiritual rewards that sacrifice brought. This chapter is
an exploration of those themes that once permeated
Christian teaching on the topic of money and possessions.
These themes provide a model of how God intends for us
to use our stuff and the vital role of those possessions in
our spiritual formation. And as we proceed we will find
these leaders returning to many of the same basic principles illuminated throughout this book.

THE KESWICK VIEW

Keswick conventions began in England's Lake District in
1874 and continued through the end of the nineteenth century, spreading to other countries in the process. Those
attending the British Keswicks were from many different
denominations and traditions, from Anglican to Plymouth
Brethren and Presbyterian to Quaker. The conferences
held at Keswick were imagined as "spiritual clinics" meant
to deepen the spiritual life of professing Christians. The
goal was to produce practical spiritual growth in the lives
of attendees, and therefore speakers treated seriously the
tough questions of daily life, including the relation of
Christians to their money and possessions.

To better understand the Keswick view of life, and its

implications for our own use of money and possessions, it might be helpful to travel back in time to the Lake District for one of these conferences. During the year 1898, what would those attending have learned about the nature of spirituality and their money?

Monday, July 18, 1898, was the first day of that year's Keswick convention. And those who had journeyed to the Lake District for spiritual refreshment would have heard the Reverend Prebendary Webb-Peploe (a fixture at Keswick for many years) speak on a passage from the Old Testament. The customary aim of the conference's first message was to arouse in the hearts of hearers a sense of their own sin and failure to lay hold of the true depths of the gospel. Webb-Peploe quickly put his finger on a perennial struggle in the Christian life: "With the majority of so-called Christians, life is one long attempt at compromise. . . . In business, men say to us calmly that they must follow the line which the generality of men are following."[2] And he gave practical examples of this life of compromise shortly later:

> He [God] has had the scraps of one's time, He has had the remnants of one's money, He has had, perhaps, our cast-off clothes which were really out of fashion, and they might go to the poor because not wanted, and then credit shall be had for having clothed the poor. And this is Christianity![3]

For Christians at the turn of the last century, just as much as at the turn of our own century, giving is not a pleasant topic. Prayer is fine. Reading the Bible is fine. Going to church is fine. But oh the struggle when it comes to giving up our money and possessions. The unstated goal of Christians in any era seems to be, *Get by with giving as little as possible,* to give our "remnants." But for Webb-Peploe, giving was not to be viewed as an unpleasant aspect of the Christian life: it is a privilege for the Christian to give. He wrote of the person who tries to decide how much giving will satisfy God, "The man does not realize that this matter of giving to God, so far from being something penal, is a holy privilege."[4] Giving therefore becomes a tool for the Christian to deepen his or her spiritual life. For the Keswick teachers, giving was not something to be wrung out of its hearers with threats and commandments, but was to be won by showing the deeper spiritual life that a person could miss if satisfied with giving just the remnants.

Other speakers during that intensive week of Bible teaching and spiritual counsel took up similar themes to Webb-Peploe's. Three main aspects can be added to what we have already seen. First is the all-important concept of God's ownership of *all*, thus making humans the stewards, or trustees, of their possessions. "The [spiritually mature] Christian feels that the silver, or the gold, or the copper, or whatever the Lord has entrusted to him, is really not his own, that he is trustee and not possessor, steward and not master."[5] Since God is the true owner, and we simply trustees of our possessions, our task becomes the management of those possessions.

A second theme that cropped up that week is the importance of the small things for the spiritual life of the Christian. "Christians, what are your daily habits?" asked one speaker. The implication is that spirituality is so much more than what happens during special times of prayer and meditation. This demands that we inspect our lives for ways to better reflect God's grace. "Are our habits brought continually to our King to be made what he would have them to be?"[6]

A third Keswick theme is the need to give one's money and life completely to God. This instruction was not hedged in any uncertain terms: "I believe everything should be held in readiness to be parted with if the Lord will."[7]

The advice to give out, and give out, and give out is surprisingly radical for modern ears—at least it is not what we expect to hear these days at conferences on spirituality. But for the Keswick speakers spirituality was impossible to imagine without complete dedication of one's life to God, and dedication that did not include one's material possessions could hardly be called dedication at all.

The Keswick teaching lay behind many of the robust missionary efforts of the time. Hudson Taylor reckoned that as many as two-thirds of the missionaries with the China Inland Mission became missionaries as a result of the Keswick ministry. The Keswick convention itself supported missionaries from its proceeds—the first so supported was Amy Carmichael, who later became well-known for her work in India.[8] Giving was a tool for the spiritual life of the mature Christian, but it also functioned as a tool for reaching the world for Christ.

At the close of the 1898 Keswick convention the customary missionary meeting was held. The speaker, Mr. Inwood, asked for all missionaries, would-be missionaries, and fathers and mothers who were willing to encourage their children to go into mission work to stand. At this invitation it seemed that about half the congregation stood, and they all prayed along with the speaker: "All I have I will give."[9] That short phrase was where all Keswick teaching led.

Those dedicating their lives to serve overseas as well as those promising to give from their profits to various ministries were not motivated by fear. They found one of the less-publicized secrets of the Christian life, that out of giving flows joy or a "present delight" as one speaker put it.[10] Life is only *truly* lived when it is in full surrender to the will of God.

Keswick teaches unmistakably that spirituality cannot be imagined without the day-by-day details of life being affected. It is absurd to talk about true spiritual life without seeing its influence on how one spends money or lives. Keswick corrects the disembodied spirituality that seems to reign unchallenged in many quarters today.

JOHN WESLEY

The Keswick teachers did not invent the connection between spirituality and money. It has a long tradition, represented to some degree throughout the history of Christianity, especially during the Reformation. The reformer Martin Luther is credited with saying that a Christian goes through three conversions—the head, the heart. . . and finally the pocketbook. A predominant thread in this tapestry is John Wesley, who provides some of the clearest teaching on the Christian's use of money.

John Wesley was the founder of the Methodist denomination, but his influence was felt throughout the entire Church, and continues to be felt today. His life spanned most of the eighteenth century (1703–1791), a century whose important events included the American Revolution. It was in his strangely radical and challenging sermons that John Wesley spoke most clearly on the topic of money and the Christian life. His teaching is certainly not to be recommended for those who want to remain comfortable!

The first thing to understand about Wesley is that he was in no way against money itself, or against the emerging market economy. The introduction of money into the world is for him an example of "the wise and gracious providence of God."[11] It is not money that is the problem, but the use of it—or "the love of it," as the Bible says. And Wesley is also quick to point out all the good that comes of money rightly spent. Because of money "we may be a defense for the oppressed, a means of health to the sick, of ease to them that are in pain."[12] Money is the tool by which immeasurable good could be done.

Neither were Christians to opt for some kind of alternative lifestyle. Wesley envisioned Christians as working at jobs like everyone else, and partaking in a market economy like everyone else. This is reflected in his first rule for the Christian's use of money: *"Gain all you can."*[13] There ought to be nothing different about the occupations or work style of the Christian. Short of sacrificing family or health or religious obligations, he or she is to be industrious and use every means to succeed in business and work.

Wesley's second rule was: *"Save all you can."* This rule is not about stockpiling money, as one might guess, but meant to give Christians pause over the way they *spend* their money. Wesley's advice is to "despise delicacy and variety, and be content with what plain nature requires."[14] Wesley saw how much good money could do, and he was pained to see to what uses money was actually put. It is hard to imagine him looking kindly on all the luxury that is commonplace among American Christians. His answer for luxury is to save—not spend. "Lay out nothing to gratify the pride of life, to gain the admiration or praise of men."[15]

It is his final rule in which Wesley shows how radical he really is: "*Give all you can.*" To gain all you can and save all you can only make sense with this conclusion. A Christian *gains* and then *saves* in order that the money can be *given.* To the person who simply gains money and deposits it in a bank, Wesley says: "You may as well throw your money into the sea. . . . Not to use, is effectually to throw it away."[16] The reason for all the work, and the reason for all the saving, is so that more money can be given, and thus more good done in the world.

Wesley's ground for giving is found in the idea of stewardship, just as it was for William Law who influenced Wesley and for the Keswick teachers who followed a hundred years later. What Wesley means by *steward* is a particular kind of servant—one who has been entrusted with personal talents, money, and possessions. The steward is responsible to God for the use of those gifts—they are not ours to enjoy for our own comfort, but ours to use "according to the particular directions which he has given us in his Word."

Wesley sees giving as something a Christian does "over and above" the general Christian duties. It is something that is absolutely essential if the Christian life is understood correctly. *All* that we have is given us by God, and since we have been entrusted with these possessions, we are responsible to use them in ways that bring Him glory. That applies to our mind, our body, our talents . . . and also our money.[17]

It is worthwhile to stop and think about how Wesley's teachings would look in modern life. Some readers may think that perhaps a person who is rich can give out like that, but ordinary folks are just barely paying their bills—how can they be expected to give? And Wesley would at first agree with this objection. The very first duty of every person is in providing for his own health: "food to eat, raiment to put on, whatever nature moderately requires for preserving the body in health and strength."[18] And second, every person is to provide these same things for all his dependents. For people who are in the position of barely managing to pay for their food, rent, utilities, and car bills, Wesley would understand if they gave little or nothing. They are taking care of their primary obligations as stewards, and nothing more needs to be said.

But while Wesley would speak compassionately for all those truly in need, he might be amused at how widespread this line of defense has become. Everyone, from those making $10,000 a year to those making $100,000, seems to feel that they are just getting by and cannot afford to give. And it is one of the laws of life that one's financial obligations rise at the exact rate of one's financial earnings. By his rule, "Save all you can," Wesley meant that Christians should find ways to live without expensive luxuries and find ways to do without what other people see as necessities.

Wesley would classify most American Christians as "rich" (his standard of wealth was quite a bit lower than most modern definitions of the word). Many people who are "barely making it" might be surprised to find themselves in this category: "Whoever has sufficient food to eat and raiment to put on, with a place where to lay his head, and something over, is *rich*."[19] This "something over" is especially important for Wesley—it is the part that a person is responsible to give away. He accepts the fact that people must provide for themselves and family, both now and in the future. He also accepts the need for business people to save the money necessary to carry on a business. But the idea of gaining money and resources for the sake of piling up wealth is incompatible with the Christian life: Money is an instrument of good; everything over and above legitimate needs should be given.

It does not take much reflection to see that this cuts radically against the grain of capitalist society. Indeed, Wesley is directly countering the teachings he found in the capitalist's bible, *The Wealth of Nations,* by Adam Smith. He takes direct aim at the accumulation of capital, and proposes in its place an alternative system based on giving away one's resources. Selflessness was to be the organizing principle of Christians; selfishness was the domain of the world.

Wesley himself realized how unpopular this kind of teaching would be, how hard to accept. He asks rhetorically at the start of his sermon on "The Danger of Riches": "Who preaches this? Great is the company of preachers at this day, regular and irregular. But who of them all openly and explicitly preaches this strange doctrine? I do not remember that in threescore years I have heard one sermon preached upon this subject."[20] And today a Christian could wonder the same thing. The topic of money and giving has become the great silent subject in the church today. To read Wesley's sermons is to hear a voice crying in the wilderness for Christians to subject *all* their life — even their stuff—to the lordship of Christ.

We also must be attentive to what is *not* found in Wesley's sermons. He never tells Christians to tithe from their earnings—he even speaks disparagingly of this practice. For Wesley to speak about a tithe would be like saying that Christians must give 10 percent, but can do with the other 90 percent just as they please. The Christian life is not about finding rules that will satisfy God's requirements, but about living wholly and completely as trustees of the possessions He gives. The tithe can certainly be a good mark for the Christian to aim for, but it should never let the Christian lose sight of the deeper command of the Christian life for complete commitment.

Wesley's goal was to build spiritually mature Christians, and he realized that balancing one's use of money and possessions would always be a tension. On the one hand, money and the concerns that come with being "rich" could strangle the spiritual life of the soul. Speaking of people who accumulate wealth Wesley writes: "Of those who thus enter into temptation very few escape out of it. And the few that do are sorely scorched by it."[21] Through all his years as a roaming evangelist and preacher, this truth had become quite obvious to him.

The real crux of Wesley's message is not to warn Christians of the dangers of riches, but to point them to giving as a Christian spiritual discipline. In his sermon entitled "A More Excellent Way," Wesley takes his listeners on a path toward practical holiness. The sermon title comes from the choice that each Christian has: to take the lower road and live in the manner of most Christians, or to take the higher road—which is more difficult—and scale spiritual heights to which God has called us. This latter road requires a certain degree of self-denial, but its rewards far outweigh the sacrifices. Wesley goes on to list some of the disciplines by which a Christian may walk on this more excellent road. They include rising early in the morning, regular prayer, doing one's work diligently, eating moderately, godly conversation . . . and the use of money.[22]

BEING FREE OF SELF

For American Christians at the start of the twenty-first century, reading John Wesley and others can be a disorienting experience. The ties between American business life and modern Christianity go unquestioned. But there was a time when Christians questioned the underpinnings of the American economic life. These radical teachers were not political activists, least of all socialists or communists. They simply believed in a radical form of the Christian life, and urged Christians not to conform to the world.

One such teacher was Charles Grandison Finney (1792–1875), one of America's great nineteenth-century revivalists. In 1836 and 1837 he delivered a series of lectures in New York called "Lectures to Professing Christians." Collected together in a book, the lectures form a practical look at what it means to live the Christian life. In one of these lectures he addresses the topic of conformity to the world. His very first point is to condemn conformity in the world of business: "The whole course of business in the world is governed and regulated by the maxims of supreme and unmixed selfishness." A few sentences later he becomes even more radical: "The whole system recognizes only the love of self. Go through all the ranks of business-men, from the man that sells candy at the sidewalk at the corner of the street, to the greatest wholesale merchant or importer in the United States, and you will find that one maxim runs through the whole — TO BUY AS CHEAP AS YOU CAN, AND SELL AS DEAR AS YOU CAN — TO LOOK OUT FOR NUMBER ONE."[23] The picture Finney draws is of a world enslaved to selfish and self-serving demands, and an economic system that praises and rewards such selfishness.

The life of the Christian, as painted by Finney, is a steady breaking free of the demands of the "self" or the sinful nature. Our greatest example is Jesus Christ, who exemplified a "spirit of self-denial, of benevolence, of sacrificing himself to do good to others."[24] For Finney, this did not mean breaking away from the world to live in some Christian commune, but living a life in the world, not of it. A person should hold a job and partake in the life of commerce, but his values and lifestyle should be radically different. Instead of "looking out for number one," the true follower of Christ finds ways to give out, give out, give out — both in terms of time and money.

Even among Christians who attend church and believe, there is still a need to make a further step of complete dedication to God's will. Phoebe Palmer (1807–1884), a highly influential Methodist writer and teacher, spoke clearly about this needed change. She called it "putting *all* on the altar." It was a phrase she could easily have derived from Romans 12:1 (NRSV), where Paul calls for Christians "to present [their] bodies as a living sacrifice." Palmer used this image to sum up the entire Christian life, and was explicit that this "all" included a Christian's money and possessions. A Christian should be able to solemnly say the following confession:

> In the name of the triune Deity, Father, Son, and
> Holy Spirit, I do hereby consecrate body, soul,
> and spirit, time, talents, influence, family, and
> estate—all with which I stand connected, near or
> remote, to be for ever, and in the most unlimited
> sense, THE LORD'S.[25]

Like the Keswick teachers and Wesley, Palmer does not set herself the task of laying down rules for the Christian to follow—no tithe or benchmarks. The exact working out of this sacrifice is for each Christian to decide in his own heart.

Her extensive journals—kept since she was a teenager—show her gradual realization of the need for complete dedication to God. Unfortunately for Palmer, it was largely as a result of tragedy that her eyes were lifted away from the world. The death of her child in a fire prompted the following sentences in her diary: "Never before have I felt such a deadness to the world, and my affections so fixed on things above. God takes our treasures to heaven, that our hearts may be there also."[26] As a result of her loss, Palmer renewed her dedication and zeal for doing "work for Jesus." This movement from tragedy to spiritual dedication is parallel to the experience of Anne Bradstreet, related at the beginning of this chapter. Both women had their eyes opened by tragedy to the way the earthly, material world had blinded them to the need for deeper spiritual commitment. It is their desire that we should learn the same.

Hannah Whitall Smith (1832–1911) wrote several Christian bestsellers in the latter half of the nineteenth century. Although a Quaker, she has many of the same emphases as the other Christian leaders we have examined thus far. She does not speak of "laying all on the altar" as does Palmer. Instead she explains the surrendered Christian life like this: "Be glad and eager to throw yourself into His loving arms, and to hand over the reins of government to

Him."[27] The metaphor is different but the idea is clearly the same: control of one's life is to be given to God. And this, again, has obvious financial implication for the believer. "We must no longer look upon our money as our own, but as belonging to the Lord, to be used in His service."[28] So once again, spiritual concerns have spilled over into the concrete life of the believer . . . to an uncomfortably radical degree.

One of Hannah Whitall Smith's book chapters is entitled "The Joy of Obedience"—and that perfectly sums up her attitude toward the Christian life. To the one who could not quite bring himself to "hand over the reins of government," she has this encouragement: "You little know, dear hesitating soul, of the joy you are missing." And that could be the word for those now reading this chapter. The demands of teachers like Wesley and Finney sound difficult because they cut so strongly against the grain of American life and the inherent selfishness of human beings. But at the end of the road is deep spiritual joy that comes from finding the "more excellent way." The selfish life could be compared to riding all day in a cramped train with shades pulled down over all the windows. The spiritual life would then be like stepping out of that train into the light-speckled landscape of the English Lake District, the clouds running past overhead and the deep blue of the lakes shining in the distance.

CHAPTER SIX

How Did We Get Here?

In the Christian community today, there is more blindness, rationalization, and unclear thinking about money than anything else.

—RANDY ALCORN[1]

I RECALL AS A CHILD ONE OF THE FIRST BACKPACKING TRIPS IN THE Pacific Northwest with my mother, father, and two older sisters. For several days, mostly in the cold, dripping rain—surrounded by clouds and fog—we wound our way up the side of a long river valley and then onto mountain switchbacks, always thinking we would reach our destination if we went just a little further. Eventually, the trail started to narrow and became overgrown with wet vegetation that soaked our boots. Soon it was covered by snow as we gained elevation. Wet and exhausted, we gave up and began the long walk out in increasingly heavy rain. It wasn't until we returned to the trailhead that we figured out we had started up the wrong trail from the very beginning.

In examining the trailhead choices, the trail we took was the most visible; it was the widest, most appealing, and most used. It looked like the correct path. However, across the parking lot was a small sign marking the trail we should have taken. It would have led us to our intended destination!

Similarly, Jesus gives us a choice in how we use our possessions as a key component of our spiritual formation. It is a choice of a life wasted on the wrong trail in pursuit of wealth on earth, or a life invested in our eternal soul.

The choice we make is a serious one because it has the ability to influence the very course of eternity and the state of our soul beyond life on this earth.

Like our family choosing the wrong trail, to a large degree, the church and Christians today are on the wrong trail when it comes to their stuff. Just as today's culture has become more materialistic and has redefined itself without God, culture has also redefined our use of possessions without God. As a result of this concession, God's Word is being diminished, our souls are not growing as they should, and the church's ability to witness to the world is weakened. Evidence of this decline shows up in several ways: Christians are failing to reverse the culture[2]; Christians have become theologically thin[3]; giving to denominations is declining[4]; and church attendees giving per capita is declining.[5] Poor use of possessions is resulting in a growing compartmentalization between faith and finances and a growing decline in all giving.[6]

Churches, seminaries, and Christian colleges seldom address issues of faith and finances; and debt is at an all-time high ($1.46 trillion at the end of the year 2000). Furthermore, eight out of ten Christians do not give at the 10 percent level, do not believe they could give at that level, and do not have the practical knowledge needed to give at that level.[7]

The previous chapter demonstrated how Christians of the past believed there to be a vital link between spiritual maturity and our possessions. How did we get so far off that path today? When did we get derailed and blinded on this subject so vital to God? Our loss of direction apparently has come upon us as a frog in a kettle. (We've all heard of how a frog can swim contentedly in a slowly heating kettle until, unaware of the gradual temperature change, it dies.) I have found in my own life that once I understood the cultural forces that put me on the wrong trail, I was able to start to alter my course. Unfortunately, little has been written about the long-term influence of a changing culture on our motives for use of possessions.

To gain this perspective, it is helpful to see how attitudes have changed over time.

Needless to say, we did not simply wake up one day to find that the economic values of our culture had changed. The values we live with are the result of a long period of cultural shifts. A good place to start is to understand this slide from the perspective of American history. Peter Dobkin Hall's book *Inventing the Nonprofit Sector*, as outlined by David L. McKenna,[8] helps trace the turning points over the past 250 years, and shows us how we arrived where we are today. The conclusion? Our charity—or what we do with our stuff—is inseparable from our culture, our character, and our soul.[9]

Two basic questions help direct us through the journey of understanding the influence of cultural change upon our use of possessions—"Why?" and "How?" A fundamental starting point is to note that three primary motivations exist for giving: (1) to benefit us personally; (2) to help others; and (3) to show stewardship to God. While all of these motives may entwine, it is assumed that one of the three will be the main driving force.

Back to the culture at large, let's consider how our giving philosophy has changed since American colonial days. These shifts reflect the changing answer that our culture gives for the question "Why do we give?" The three main periods we will be considering in this chapter are: (1) Stewardship, 1740–1840; (2) Philanthropy, 1850–1950; and (3) Development/Self-centered, 1950 to the present. Again, while recognizing that these ways of giving entwine and overlap in our history, one of these three answers dominates within each period and probably reflects your attitude today.

THE STEWARDSHIP PERIOD

While it is debatable whether the United States can be called a "Christian nation" (even though 87 percent list themselves as Christians), the fundamental fact is that Americans are a people with deep Christian roots. Such phrases as "endowed by our Creator with certain inalienable rights" and "in God we trust" are not idle words. Personal and corporate faith in God permeated the life of our founders with the attitude and motive of biblical stewardship. They believed that: (1) God provides all our resources; (2) God entrusts us with the responsibility to manage these resources; and (3) God holds each of us accountable for the way we use the resources He has entrusted to us. To our Puritan ancestors, in particular, money was major among the resources to which they applied the stewardship test. This attitude became so pervasively engrained in early American culture that the Stewardship period continued from the founding of our nation well into the 1850s.

This Stewardship period was built on three intertwining roots: (1) the ideological root of biblical stewardship; (2) the democratic ideal of the common good; and (3) the Puritan ethic of responsible piety.

The ideological root of biblical stewardship was planted by our founding forefathers and mothers, whose "biblical vision for the moral community" made personal redemption and social responsibility inseparable. Just before the Pilgrims disembarked from the *Mayflower* to establish the Plymouth Colony, they heard this biblical vision enunciated in a sermon by their governor, John Winthrop. He preached:

> We must delight in each other, make others' condition our condition, rejoice together, mourn together, labor and suffer together, always having before our eyes our community as members of the same body.

From that sermon came the vision that America would be a "City on a Hill" and a light to the nations.

Alongside this ideological taproot grew the political root, the democratic ideal of the "common good." Thomas Jefferson, an avowed deist, offered this ideal as the humanistic alternative for the biblical vision of the moral community. Realistically, however, Jefferson's democratic idea depended upon the biblical vision for its moral grounding.

With these first two strands grew the economic root of the Puritan ethic. Usually referred to as the "Puritan work ethic" because of its emphasis on industrious labor, we cannot forget that the Puritans also preached "responsible prosperity" with accountability to God for the blessing of wealth.

Generally, from the colonial period until the Civil War, the church took the lead in charitable work as evidence of its stewardship. Schools, hospitals, orphanages, and missions of mercy symbolized the American response to the needs of the illiterate, impoverished, sick, and lonely masses. As Nathan Hatch has written in his book *The Democratization of American Christianity,* a revived church has always been "remarkably effective in forging moral communities among the poor, sick, ignorant, and elderly—the most vulnerable people on earth."[10]

Revitalization in the 1740s and 1750s came through the spiritual renewal of the first Great Awakening, spurred by Jonathan Edwards and George Whitefield. Personal redemption fed social responsibility, and the taproot of the biblical vision of the moral community was kept alive. Alexis de Tocqueville, the French historian, caught the spirit of Christian stewardship when, after witnessing a barn raising that engaged the energies of the whole community, he wrote, "America has the soul of a church."[11] While traces of this period are evident today, it gave way to a new giving philosophy in the mid-nineteenth century.

THE PHILANTHROPIC PERIOD

A gradual but significant shift away from the biblical stewardship worldview started as America became more urbanized, industrialized, and capitalized. The Carnegies and Rockefellers accumulated massive fortunes and established the first foundations. They also embraced the concept of philanthropy (meaning "friend of humankind") as distinct from stewardship ("servant of God"). The change speaks for itself. In the Philanthropic period, the ideological, political, and economic roots were radically altered.

The ideological root of Social Darwinism took the place of the biblical vision for the moral community. Credit for wealth was given to good fortune rather than to God, and philanthropic gifts went to the "selective good" rather than the "common good." Professional philanthropy replaced personal stewardship and focused upon social reconstruction more than individual redemption. Rather than helping people succeed in society through charity, the focus shifted to remaking society, with giving serving as a catalyst for political, economic, and social change.

The prophet for the Philanthropic period was Andrew Carnegie. In his essay entitled "The Gospel of Wealth," he explained his own good fortune as evidence of natural selection and survival of the fittest among the human species. With one swift stroke, Carnegie cut the taproot of biblical stewardship and adopted what he called "scientific philanthropy" based upon Darwinian theory. He attacked boldly the indiscriminate charity of Christian stewardship by saying, "It is better for mankind that the millions (of dollars) of the rich were thrown into the sea than to encourage the slothful, the drunken, the unworthy."[12]

Carnegie went another step by redefining the democratic ideal of the common good. He wrote, "The best means of benefiting the community is to place within its reach ladders upon which the aspiring can rise." With these words, he drew the line of distinction between those who were worthy of charity and those who were not. The "selective good" replaced the root of the "common good."

Severing the third root of the Puritan ethic followed naturally. In place of "responsible prosperity," Carnegie espoused an "entrepreneurial ethic," putting charity on a business basis. According to him, the motive of philanthropy was not response to human suffering, but calculated cost benefit for continuous economic growth with the redistribution of wealth to sustain free enterprise.

As radical and as selfish as this may seem, Carnegie

recognized that his giving would be interpreted by the general public as a continuation of Christian stewardship to which we still gave lip service. Mark Twain, however, in his 1889 black comedy, *A Connecticut Yankee in King Arthur's Court,* criticized Carnegie's motivation to use charity to benefit the industrial complex as nothing more than an instrument for enlarging the "destructive capacity of the human race."[13] When philanthropy is motivated to help only people who are a good business investment, charity becomes a form of exploitation. Ironically, by secularizing the process of giving, the seeds of this philosophy's own decay were sown.

In the midst of this period shift from Stewardship to Philanthropic, the second Great Awakening, led by Charles Finney, occurred in the mid-1880s. As a result of this spiritual renewal, redeemed men and women founded voluntary associations across the country to meet human needs that could not be met by the church alone. Among them were the YMCA and the YWCA, followed later by the Red Cross and United Appeal (now United Way).

Even President Abraham Lincoln, despite his preoccupation with the Civil War, reflected on this steady erosion of values when in 1863 he called for a National Day of Fasting, Humility, and Prayer. In a speech he said:

We have grown in numbers, wealth and power, as no other nation has ever grown. But we have forgotten God. We have vainly imagined, in the deceitfulness of our hearts, that all these bless-ings were produced by some superior wisdom and virtue of our own.

By the end of the century, Carnegie's concept of giving based upon social Darwinism with its elitist mentality, selective philanthropy, and economic cost benefits came under challenge in a best-selling novel by Charles Sheldon entitled, *In His Steps.* In the book he tells about a "dusty, worn, shabby-looking young man" who stumbles into the morning worship of the Reverend Henry Maxwell's wealthy downtown church. In a calm voice, he rises in the service to say, "I'm not an ordinary tramp, though I don't know of any teaching of Jesus that makes one kind of tramp less worthy from saving than another, do you?" He then explains that he is a printer by trade who lost his job to a linotype machine ten months ago. For three days now, he has tramped through their city in search of a job and a word of encouragement. Without bitterness or rancor, he asks the question, "What do you mean when you sing, 'I'll go with Him, with Him, all the way?' Do you mean that you are suffering and denying yourselves? Are you trying to save the lost and suffering humanity as I understand Jesus did?" Then he tells about his wife dying in a tenement owned by a member of the church and asks again, "I wonder if following Jesus was true in his case?" With that, the tramp falls forward and dies on the communion table. From that point on, the meaning of Christian discipleship for that church changes dramatically. Once again, discipleship means stewardship and stewardship means self-sacrifice for the needy, whether or not they are deemed worthy. The people of the congregation ask only one question as they confront the needs of their community, "What would Jesus do?"[14]

The problem was not in the practice of business itself—but rather the lack of response from the church. Francis Schaeffer wrote:

> If industrialization had been accompanied by a strong emphasis on the compassionate use of accumulated wealth and on the dignity of each individual, the industrial revolution would have indeed been a revolution for good. But all too often . . . the church was silent . . . on a compassionate use of wealth. . . . Following Industrialization non-compassionate use of wealth became commonplace.[15]

Time has only magnified these earlier secular tendencies.

We live in a culture that worships at the shrine of four related idols: pleasure, wealth, professional status, and physical appearance. It is a culture of convenience rather than duty and of avoiding pain rather than seeking to relieve the burdens of others. To what extent have the idols of this age—materialism, smug professionalism, and the quest for self—influenced our search for the good life above knowing God? John Wesley expressed his profound concern, "I fear as riches have increased, the essence of religion has decreased in the same proportion."

The cultural drift at this point is well established, but the influence continues to play itself out today.

The Development or Self-centered Period

The continuing shift in the motives and means of using possessions was very evident around the 1950s when fund-raising became big business and development became a career. Spurred by tax law changes, the boom in computers, accessibility of telephones, and relatively inexpensive third-class mail, the number of foundations has increased from 12,500 to more than one million today.

Certainly there continued to be evidence of the "moral community," "the common good," and the "ladder of opportunity," but the "managerial motive" of the fund-raising industry became the *modus operandi* for the Development efforts. More interest is shown in research into the causes of human suffering than its relief. Seed grants for innovative proposals have replaced sustaining grants for programs, and accounting for efficiency seems more important than reporting for effectiveness. Business giving more and more reflects what is advantageous for the firm.

Christian organizations were quick to adopt the titles, motives, and methods of secular fund-raisers. Many people working for Christian organizations in the 1940s and 1950s held the title "stewardship representative" and viewed their work as ministry. One example is chronicled in Robert D. Noles' book *Water Boy!*, in which he talked about his "stewardship work" at Wheaton College in terms of ministry to the people he "served." He would pray each morning to see who the Lord would put on his heart to visit and encourage in biblical stewardship giving![16]

Later, as the Bob Noles of Christian organizations became viewed as outdated and inefficient, they were replaced with field representatives, planned-giving officers, or other such names, and their work was shifted to a "sales basis" from a "ministry basis." Computer printouts started to provide their calling lists, and prayer often took a backseat.

Mixed with this managerial motive is the political root of governmental involvement, regulating the means of giving through fiscal and legal statutes. Despite the fact that Ronald Reagan campaigned on the promise to restore the "biblical vision of the moral community" through voluntary agencies, and George Bush championed a "thousand points of light" through individual action, the irony is that charitable organizations became more and more dependent upon regulated federal dollars during the 1980s. That trend accelerated even further in the 1990s. As strange as it seems, up to 60 percent of today's charitable dollar comes from the federal government, and President Clinton's era encouraged an increase in that percentage. We can understand the frustration of Robert Goheen, former President of Princeton University and later President of the Council on Foundations, when he wrote, "Has charity become all law? Is it irrevocably committed to legal practitioners?"[17] If he is right, the roots of managerial motives and legally regulated means have once again redefined the meaning of giving into the process of development.

Foundations do not hesitate to state specifically or tacitly the driving force of "self-interest" behind their gifts. A clear example of this shift is the ARCO foundation that stopped giving for the benefit of the community and shifted instead to what benefited the business or its employees. The carryover also affects the way in which individuals use their possessions as a reflection of our changing culture.

Perhaps this prevailing attitude accounts for the popularity of incentives for donors to give. Direct mail gimmicks, giving clubs, premiums, and tax benefits are used to appeal to the self-interest of the prospective giver. The practices of giving and asking for money today reflect the character values of our culture. Robert Wuthnow has written in his book, *Acts of Compassion,* our new attitude toward charitable giving "allows us to carve up our caring into little chunks that require only a level of giving that does not conflict with our needs and interests as individuals."[18] In this self-centered Development period, we volunteer time and give money as a convenient choice that preserves our freedom, meets our needs, and protects our schedule. We have almost completely separated how we use our possessions from our spiritual life.

REVITALIZING THE RELIGIOUS ROOTS OF GIVING

We now understand how the biblical vision of the moral community, the democratic ideal of the common good, and the Puritan ethic of responsible prosperity have given way to the motive of self-interest, the goal of the public good, and the means of self-benefit. Nowhere within the current paradigm do we find a place for the eternal soul.

Today, the term *stewardship* generally has lost all spiritual meaning. The environmentalists use the word to denote care of the earth, and secular fund-raisers refer to good stewardship as making sure a person is appropriately thanked for a gift and that the gift is used for the purpose designated by the donor.

In Robert Wuthnow's three-year study on religious and economic values, 89 percent of the respondents agreed, "Our society is much too materialistic," 74 percent said materialism is a serious social problem, and 71 percent said society would be better off if less emphasis were placed on money.[19] Yet, while we see materialism in our neighbors and decry its presence on television or in the movies, we do not seem to be able to find it in our own hearts. Lifestyles of those within the church vary little—if at all—from the lifestyle of others in the same income bracket.

Even more alarming is the fact that the church as a

whole is allowing its voice to be silenced by the surrounding culture. Partially from the old fear of sounding as if all the church wants is money, and partially because of greater confusion as to what the Bible really does teach about money, pastors have shied away from speaking out on economic issues and their connection to core spiritual values. And secular approaches to fund-raising have emerged to fill the void even in our churches. Christian stewardship—that biblical approach practiced by the Puritans—is seldom even mentioned today, let alone taught or practiced. It is no accident that at a time when the church is becoming fractured and culturally feeble, the values of Christian stewardship are also being neglected.

Where do we go from here? Some may say, "Americans give more than $203 billion a year to charity, more than any other nation, and the largest percentage goes to religion. What's the problem?" Others may note that we are moving into a time when the largest transfer of wealth in the history of the world—as much as $100 trillion—will pass from one generation to the next. If all this is true, why raise these issues?

It seems, however, that there is concern from many fronts. Robert Payton, retired President of the Center on Philanthropy, states the following in the book *The Responsibilities of Wealth*: "The strength of American giving is based upon its religious origins and values and traditions. Philanthropy as we know it today may not survive a serious deterioration of its religious values."[20] Note he uses the word *philanthropy* as synonymous with giving. Jacob Riis, in his book, *How the Other Half Lives*, sees philanthropy as "a bridge founded upon justice and built of human hearts."[21] Peter Dobkin Hall, a student of nonprofit organizations at Yale, follows Riis's words with this conclusion, "Without discovering its religious roots, American giving is unlikely to play a significant role in building such a bridge."[22] In summary, unless we rediscover our religious roots, the distinctive American character of giving and asking for money will be lost.

The key question for the church today, according to Robert Bellah, is "whether our organized religion can offer a genuine alternative to tendencies that are deeply destructive in our current pattern of institutions or whether religious institutions are simply one more instance of the problem."[23] As for individuals in our churches, Bellah says that the critical question is whether we are loyal to the divine mission of the church or simply use it as an "instrument for self-fulfillment and abandon it as soon as it doesn't meet our needs."[24]

The message is clear from the secular prophets; now hear Isaiah the prophet of God speak on the issue. He draws a direct line from righteousness to justice and mercy in his prophecy to Israel. If righteousness prevails, there is justice for all people and compassion for the needy. If righteousness is lost, oppression of the weak and neglect of the needy is the inevitable outcome. We, as a nation and as a church, cannot escape that truth.

Are you on the wrong trail? Have you been swallowed up by culture? Or, is your use of possessions tied to your soul? If so, you have a life-and-death stake in the recovery of our biblical roots, for it seems clear that a moral vision for the common good by prosperous people cannot be sustained otherwise. The first Great Awakening of the eighteenth century planted those roots; the second Great Awakening of the nineteenth century kept those roots alive; and though they withered in the twentieth century, they are not yet dead.

The big unknown is who will make a difference and realize that our possessions are a tool, a test, and a trademark? Which Christians are willing to examine the materialistic pull of our culture upon their eternal souls and set out on a countercultural journey of spiritual formation that will point their souls toward God? It is clear that the gospel of Jesus urges us to be at the leading edge of culture. Even though culture has great influence, it appears that there is always time for us to put God and His teaching first.

The next few chapters provide guidance on how to master this cultural maze and work on your spiritual formation. You will learn how to deal with appeals and what to expect of your church, family, and Christian educational institutions as you attempt to keep on the path of linking your possessions and your soul.

CHAPTER SEVEN

When Everyone Has Their Hands Out

Giving is primarily a spiritual matter . . . an act of obedient worship . . . the spiritual growth of supporters should be the primary concern of every Christian fundraiser.

—R. Scott Rodin[1]

A MODERN-DAY FACT OF LIFE IS THAT YOU ARE BOMBARDED WITH financial appeals from all sides—through the mail, at the office, on radio and television, via phone (often at dinnertime) and e-mail, at the market, and on the front porch from neighbor children. The list could go on and on. Whether you realize it or not, the manner in which these appeals are made affect your spiritual formation, both consciously and unconsciously. It is estimated that there are well over a million nonprofit organizations in the United States alone. Most of these organizations, churches included, are dependent on gift income to stay solvent and thus they aggressively try to raise as much money as they can. Unfortunately, few organizations ever try to grow your soul and prioritize your spiritual formation.

How should a wise steward of God's resources respond in this high-pressure environment? Assuming the primary purpose of your giving is to worship God and develop an intimate relationship with Him, how do you keep from letting aggressive appeals negatively influence your eternal soul?

The focus of this chapter is to help you become a more strategic steward by: (1) developing a system to constructively handle the external pressure of appeals; (2) forming a plan that allows you to be intentional and strategic about your giving; and (3) learning how to respond to fund-raisers' approaches so that they do not negatively affect your desire to grow your eternal soul.

At the outset, it is important to acknowledge that you are in control of what you do. You do not need to succumb to pressure, however intense. One of the best ways to handle pressure is to adopt a system that allows you to intentionally and strategically monitor your giving. That way you'll have a framework to address all types and sizes of requests that come your way.

INTENTIONALLY FOCUSING OUR GIVING

Most giving is done impulsively, often out of guilt of the moment. In fact, an estimated 70 percent of giving is impulsive, 20 percent out of habit, 7 percent thoughtful, and just 3 percent careful or intentional.[2] The goal of a systematic approach is to reduce impulsive giving and increase strategic giving that builds your soul concerns.

The suggested process, adapted from Alan Youngren's work,[3] is comprised of five steps, which build on one another (see chart 7-1). The combined answers to these questions provide a total approach in your giving.

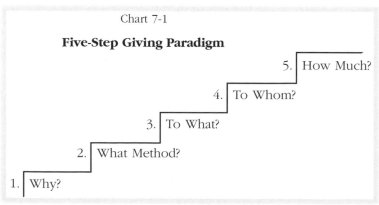

Chart 7-1

Five-Step Giving Paradigm

5. How Much?

4. To Whom?

3. To What?

2. What Method?

1. Why?

1. *Why?*—Determine your motives.
2. *What method?*—Establish your methodology.
3. *To what?*—Clarify areas of interest.
4. *To whom?*—List recipients that meet your predetermined objectives.
5. *How much?*—Estimate an amount or range.

Let's take a closer look at each of these steps.

1. Determine and Understand Your Motives for Giving

The first step is to have a clear understanding of your motives for giving. The hope is that by this point in the book, you desire to seek and follow a biblical worldview in giving, that you accept the vital link between your eternal soul and your earthly possessions.

As developed in the preceding chapters, your giving is a choice of kingdoms (see chart 3-2). If you are following God's kingdom, you give out of heartfelt thanks to God, as a steward of His resources. This critical and countercultural foundational decision sets the stage for the other four steps.

2. Establish Your Methodology of Giving

Once you know in your mind and heart why you give, the next step is to determine your method. Giving money involves several considerations. While in *accumulating* money you are preparing to have an effect, in *dispersing* money you are actually having an effect.

The wise steward generally seeks to support effective and efficient causes and to make those recipients more effective and efficient through support. To accomplish this, it is wise to avoid two pitfalls common in giving. The first of these is "dilution of effect," which is the result of the proliferation of small gifts. The logical approach to combating this pitfall is to give fewer small gifts and more large ones. As Harold Seymour points out in his classic, *Designs for Fund-Raising,* the average giver has the "mental room" to maintain an active interest in the work of approximately six organizations.[4] If he or she would focus support to approximately six to ten ministries, then the chances of being more strategic and intentional would increase.

Unfortunately, many givers have difficulty refusing any appeal for funds. The result is many small gifts (the average gift to a Christian cause is less than $50). This "shotgun" approach makes it difficult for the giver to really know the organizations being supported; and it reduces effectiveness by as much as one half of these small gifts going to processing costs.

As you can understand, processing costs are multiplied many times by small gifts. The cost of receiving and processing a gift does not vary with its size, because the processing procedure is the same regardless. A gift must be entered in a number of records, deposited in the bank, and the donor sent a receipt. This means that the recipient organization pays as much to process a $25 gift as it pays to process a $10,000 gift. Consequently, processing takes a bigger bite out of a small gift than it does out of a larger one. Consider accumulating all the money you will give to a single organization or project and send it less frequently, if at all possible. If you give to six organizations, you can give twice a year to all rather than to each organization every month.

The key to coordinating the accumulation and dispersal lies in planning. Begin your giving year by listing your proposed gifts, noting the order in which you will make them and the size of each. Quite naturally, a list of your gifts from the previous year probably dominates this new list. Perhaps you are a steward newly convinced of the value of truly knowing those to whom you give and have just finished gathering information about potential recipients; perhaps you are a steward experienced in these matters and thoroughly committed to a list of six to ten recipients. Whatever your situation, you should accumulate funds until you have enough for the first gift on your list, and then make that gift. In this way you will give systematically and intentionally to every organization on your list.

If you cannot accurately forecast your income, the

resulting difficulty lies not in compiling your list, but in determining the size of each gift. For those who have this difficulty but still want to use a dispersal list in order to give money uniformly over a twelve-month period, here are three approaches to the problem:

- Start by listing your prospective recipients in order of importance, putting the organization to which you are most committed first (possibly your church), and maintain that pattern. Then put an amount next to each name on the list—an amount representing what you will give that recipient if your income for the year turns out to be close to your estimate. What you are then saying to yourself is, "I am not going to give organizations lower on the list anything until I have accumulated designated dollars for organization number one, designated dollars for number two, and so on."
- Delay sending any gifts until you can quite accurately estimate your income for the year (but don't delay putting money aside).
- Send donations to your entire list quarterly or semiannually, if possible.

A final value is maintaining commitment over time. This is a strategic matter that warrants attention because of the consistent support it provides an organization.

It is important to realize that your commitment is a very real part of your support. Organizations need to know they can count on you. If support were constant, many organizations could reduce expenses by not sending as many appeals. You maintain your commitment—and demonstrate it—by two means: *consistency* and *continuity*.

Consistency involves timing, a determinant factor in successful cash-flow management within the organizations you support. Your annual gift (remember that a single gift per year is the easiest on their processing capacities) ideally would reach the recipient at a similar time each year.

The more an organization's support comes from committed stewards making predictable gifts, the more efficient that organization can be. And you help maintain that efficiency when you inform them of any change in your giving style.

Continuity means an uninterrupted flow of support—in real dollars—at an established level. This involves caring for two additional provisions:

- *Adjustments for inflation.* One way to handle adjustments for inflation is to assign each of your recipients a percentage of your total giving, and as your income increases, their percentage of it increases accordingly.
- *Giving beyond your earthly life.* The principle here is not that money should continue flowing indefinitely to your recipients. However, you may want to grant a portion of your estate, to be distributed, after your life on earth. With appreciated assets common in today's economy, this is an important area to consider in your giving.

A final point is how to deal with earnest letters coming from those you support, carrying news of an unexpected crisis or opportunity, and asking for a special gift. What about the planning for such "emergencies"? Here are two suggestions: First, if these crisis/opportunity messages did not work so well, you would not receive so many of them. Those asking for money know they can raise more money from crisis appeals, so sometimes they will "create a crisis." Don't be part of the reason that a crisis appeal works. Notice how many coincide nicely with the end of the sender's fiscal year. Research crisis appeals carefully, and then if you want to plan to give to unexpected requests, set up a fund. If one of your six to ten designated organizations has a legitimate crisis, you can disperse these funds toward the unplanned request without affecting your other giving.

3. Clarify Your Areas of Interest

There are literally hundreds of thousands of Christian nonprofit ministries, so without carefully defining your stewardship interests and then focusing on those interests, you will find it difficult to give effectively.

Some may question this emphasis on personal interests in giving rather than God's. However, the two are related, not opposed, especially if your concerns are bathed in prayer. God gives you these interests as stimulants to your concern. As such, they encourage you to give. In fact, it is a tribute to God's love and thoughtfulness that He directs our stewardship by giving us interests in varying areas of the work of the Great Commission. If we follow and develop these interests, they can add to our joy in giving.

In approaching this step, take your time. Identify your interests clearly, and think about them long enough to discover which ones matter most and why. Or here's another approach to getting started: Without previous reflection, pray about Christian work and Christian workers anywhere and everywhere. The activities and groups that enter your prayers most quickly are valuable indications of your true interests.

Thanks be to God that He gives one person a strong interest in Africa and another in China; that someone is primarily interested in home missions and another in telling the Word to primitive, "unreached" peoples; that one person has a passion for Christian higher education and another for rescue missions. All the work must be done, and a variety of interests is the primary insurance that it will be.

Out of a feeling that people everywhere are in real need, particularly spiritual need, some stewards support several organizations they find most effective and efficient. Other people's highest priority is the support of a particular organization or an individual. Many develop a strong allegiance to sending to organizations, supporting whatever organization sponsors the individual.

One valuable resource in choosing giving options outside the local church is the book *The Prospering*

Parachurch.[5] Its outline classifies numerous interests: arts/culture, associations, audiovisual/media, camps/conferences, constituency-based ministries, consulting, counseling/guidance, education, environment/agriculture, evangelism, health care, legal assistance/political action, missions, print media, relief, and development and social services.

A possible caution before you begin is not to attempt to identify every interest that you can uncover, but limit yourself to your strongest preferences. Often stewards will identify somewhere between six and ten interests (including their own churches). If your own number of interests does not fall within this range, remember that the *quality* of your ability to know the organizations is more important that the *quantity* of organizations you select.

It is ideal to limit yourself so that you can realistically and effectively keep up with each organization. Keep in mind that thorough stewardship is a time-consuming matter. Ideally, you will select your recipients on the basis of thorough knowledge, which means obtaining answers to detailed questions (as the next point explains)—not simply looking over the limited information that gift-seeking organizations will send you.

Finally, keep in mind that each of your gifts should be large enough to be meaningful to you. Each should be a real stimulus to your continued concern for the group receiving that gift. Supporting too many organizations means sending out a plethora of smaller gifts that will probably diminish your sense of accomplishment through your giving.

Having said all this, I am not suggesting that you toss out your current list of recipients and begin again. However, I am suggesting that you consider what may be a rather significant change in your approach to deciding who will receive your money. Go from a subjective viewpoint (determined by your interests) to an objective viewpoint (determined by your assessment of which organizations will best serve your interests). Accomplishing this change means obtaining the best information you can acquire.

4. To Whom Will You Give?

Once you have completed steps 1 through 3, the next step is to determine the specific organizations that you will support financially. Selecting actual gift recipients is a two-step procedure. The first step is *identification* (finding a usable number of candidate organizations in the field of each of your stewardship interests). The second step is *evaluation* of each of the groups you have identified.

What you are looking for in the identification process is legitimacy. In any group or community, there are those who live by the standards and morals of the group and those who don't. Does a given organization belong to an association made up of its peers? And does that association have among its membership requirements certain standards that must be followed? Or does a given group belong to the Evangelical Council for Financial Accountability (ECFA)? Feel free to call their toll-free number (1-800-323-9473) to see if an organization has been given a seal of approval.

In the second step, evaluation, the wise steward goes on the offensive. Contact the organizations that have become candidates for your support. In a letter of inquiry (sometimes this information can be found on a Web page), ask the candidate for five specific pieces of information:

- Its statement of purpose and some examples of successful past fulfillment of these purposes;
- A list of its officers and board of directors;
- Its most recent financial statement and the auditor's cover letter if the statements have been audited;
- A statement on what percentage of your gift actually is used in ministry;
- A statement of future plans for its program: special projects and, especially, permanent projects.

As a result of this information and your evaluation process, you should be able to make well-informed decisions as to the organization's credibility and match with your giving objectives. Now that you've determined the who, what, and how, the next step is how much.

5. Estimate How Much You Will Give

I have a friend who recently changed jobs and moved to another state. He and his wife made an intentional decision to structure their lifestyle so they could live on two-thirds of their income and give the remainder to God's work. This intentional approach determined other lifestyle issues, but the decision to give and the amount came first.

A steward who wishes to be strategic in the exercise of giving should begin by deciding what portion of income will be returned to God. Whether this percentage is 5 or 10 or 20 or 50 percent, it should be a predetermined figure based on the income the steward is currently receiving.

Next, the challenge is to accumulate the money and enjoy giving it away. As we all know from experience, once behind in our giving, it is hard to play catch-up. And once you're really behind, meeting your goals becomes close to impossible—unless, of course, the portion you have determined to give is not a financial challenge to you.

What can the Christian steward do to make accumulation a pillar of his giving program rather than a pitfall, a joy rather than a burden? First, he should eliminate the two most common harmful mistakes Christians make in readying money for giving—giving from what is left, and tying dispersal to income.

As mentioned in previous chapters, Scripture is clear that the primary principle guiding stewardship in the early church was that of first fruits. The key to first fruits giving is setting aside from the start that portion of your income going to the Lord's work. The idea is to "live on the rest" after God's portion is given, rather than giving to God whatever is left after you have maintained yourself "in the manner to which you have become accustomed." Sadly, the latter approach is the way most Christians manage accumulation. The first fruits approach is also an effective means of maintaining a positive attitude toward stewardship responsibilities. If you live on the remaining amount of income, you will have to tailor your lifestyle and "needs" to available dollars so that you do not consume what you originally intended for God's work.

Many people believe they should set aside (accumulate) and give (disperse) their stewardship monies the same way a baseball player in the middle of a double play should catch and then throw the ball—all in one motion.

I do not have to give away today what I set aside today. Many people have been pressed into feeling that their stewardship monies are burning a hole in their pockets by an overzealous reading of Paul's admonition in 2 Corinthians 8:11, where he urges them to "complete" or "finish" the work of providing for the saints at Jerusalem. Such zealots often translate this admonition, "Do it immediately." Be assured, however, that any group deserving support operates on an annual budget. In this context, "immediately" becomes anytime within the operating year. When you are concerned that monies be distributed as soon as they are received, you increase your vulnerability to three specific stewardship concerns:

- *Dilution of effect,* due to breaking up of a large gift into smaller monthly units.
- *The size of the gift being determined by circumstance.* If, to avoid dilution of effect, you decide that your total gift to one organization will be everything set aside in one period (say, one month), then the size of that gift is determined by circumstance (the amount available from that period) and not by careful, prayerful decision-making on your part.
- *Money on hand, but no specific recipient to give it to.* Eighteen hundred years ago, the *Didache,* a significant second-century Christian document, wisely advised believers, "Let thy alms sweat in thy hand until thou knowest to whom thou givest."[6] That advice may apply today.

It is possible, however, to make this matter seem simpler than it is. Accumulation and dispersal ideally should be coordinated. Also, there is no ideal or single best accumulation procedure. This is because stewards (like other people) receive their income in a variety of patterns. Some receive a fixed amount at regular intervals—weekly, biweekly, or monthly. Others receive varying amounts at these same regular intervals. And still others receive varying amounts at sporadic intervals.

One particularly helpful technique is to set aside "God's" money at the time you put your paycheck in the bank, before it gets mixed with the rest of your money. The simplest and most helpful manner of doing this is to set up a separate checking account for stewardship monies. The greatest value of the separate account is psychological. Most stewards find that, because this money is separated from the rest of their holdings, they no longer even think of using it for their personal needs and wants.

This tactic has significant potential for making stewardship a positive and enjoyable experience. Some stewards even find that the separate account affords a freedom akin to giving away somebody else's money, without short-circuiting the joy of sharing.

If you do not establish a separate account, at least keep some continuing written record of how much giving money is accumulating in your regular bank account. This technical separation of funds will help accomplish the goal of taking the Lord's portion "off the top," rather than giving to God from "what is left."

If you question why I make such an issue of setting aside first fruits in a disciplined manner, consider this. If accumulating your stewardship monies annually is easy for you, or if sending off an occasional check consistently adds up at year's end to what you want to give, perhaps you should challenge yourself to give at a level that would require greater sacrifice and effort. Accumulation requires this kind of effort only when you have a truly challenging goal for how much you will give.

Use the power and influence you have as a giver and write inquiries to organizations you are serious about supporting. You will gain information, and you will send them the message that only worthy groups deserve to prosper.

After you've completed each of these five steps, making decisions about giving is thoughtful, intentional, proactive, and should preserve your soul in the process.

WHAT YOU SHOULD EXPECT FROM A CHRISTIAN ORGANIZATION'S FUND-RAISING

As this book has outlined, the primary purpose of your giving is to worship God and develop an intimate relationship with Him (not to meet the funding goals of organizations).[7] From this worldview, then, the top priority of those asking you to give should be to assist you in using the tools, passing the test, and establishing your trademark as defined in chapter 1. In other words, they should: (1) educate you about biblical stewardship; (2) use methods that place your priorities of God first; and (3) communicate in a way that assists you, the giver, to put God and your spiritual formation first in the use of your possessions, not the needs of the organization.

The wise steward realizes that all these priorities of ministering to you and your soul-needs can easily get lost. For this reason, the wise steward should have high expectations of those asking for funds.

Drawing from the work of Jeavons and Basinger,[8] here are nine expectations that you should have from those who try to raise money from you:

1. The organization should acknowledge that the true purpose of giving is to build your soul (relationship with God), and that this has a higher priority than the financial needs of the organization.
2. The organization should have a written statement explaining how they will approach you, the steward of God's resources.

3. In all they do, they will have integrity and never exploit the sacred trust with you, by hiding costs or avoiding reporting failures (Mark 12:38-40).

4. The organization will take a kingdom view of God's work worldwide, allowing you relationships with other ministries that are truly cooperative rather than competitive (Philippians 4:10-13).

5. The organization will provide you with meaningful opportunities for genuine participation in the ministry (Philippians 4:14-16).

6. The organization demonstrates that it seeks out and hires spiritually mature, theologically reflective leadership for its fund resource acquisition (Matthew 6:21).

7. There is an integrated approach to the organization's program goals with its money acquisition system (Philippians 1:5; 4:13).

8. The organization encourages you to see that all your resources are temporarily entrusted to you from God, to be used and shared to promote the welfare of all of God's creation (Proverbs 24:3-4).

9. As a result of giving, you should have a sense of peace, joy, and fulfillment of accomplishing God's work as a steward, not a sense of guilt or remorse (Philippians 4:17-19; 1 Chronicles 29:9).

Since so many churches, Christian colleges, and seminaries have abdicated their stewardship teaching responsibilities, those organizations that ask for your money have the most potential to educate and influence you in this regard. Indeed, they have a high calling before God to treat you and God's resources in a way that is worthy of the One to whom the resources ultimately belong.

You should determine whether the asking organization shares your faith, attempts to have a mature, respectful relationship with you, and focuses on service to you and your need to give as unto the Lord. It should be evident that they integrate these principles into their everyday work. Recognizing that it is God who works in your heart, motivating you to give, it is the asker's responsibility to pray for you and with you to ask that this happen.

The asking organization's focus in raising funds should be to develop a lifelong relationship with you. All communications (publications, phone calls, mail, personal visits) then become an effort to build bonds of honesty and integrity and should avoid manipulative techniques, despite pressures to reach a particular goal. The giving-and-asking endeavor is a sacred trust that must be taken seriously. The asking organization's role is one of service to facilitate this trust—to provide giving opportunities, to assist in wise estate planning, and to offer counsel on total giving. Through these services, God's people are enabled to work together in providing sufficient funds for ministries.

Once you have developed a workable system to calculate your giving and understand the expectations of those seeking funds, here are eleven cautions to be aware of as you consider financial appeals:

1. Premium offers promising a return for a certain size gift.
2. Appeals detached from the spiritual basis of the organization.
3. Asking that is unconcerned with you as a partner in ministry.
4. The asking approach robs you of the joy of giving.
5. When you feel like a "means to an end."
6. Your privacy is not respected.
7. Impersonal fund-raising language is used.
8. You are promised giving class distinctions by amount given.
9. Money-raising events that are not ministry or charity focused.
10. Deceptive, emotional, or guilt-ridden asking practices.
11. Communication that does not support a stewardship approach to giving.

The intent of this chapter has been to prepare you to be a strategic steward of God's riches by: developing a giving system, having high expectations of fund-raising approaches, and alerting you to methods that can trip you up. If you absorb them as a whole, you should now be prepared to be an intentional, strategic steward, thus enhancing your relationship to God and experiencing joy from being a generous giver.

CHAPTER EIGHT

What You Should Expect from Your Church

Today's pastors are, at best, reluctant stewards of their church's human, physical, and financial resources . . . and today's seminaries, also by their own admission, are extremely reluctant to take the lead in helping pastors and other church leaders learn how to become better stewards.

—The Reluctant Steward[1]

Since how we use our possessions is an important part of our spiritual formation and ultimate state of our soul, one would expect a chain of solid Christian training in this area: seminaries teach pastors, pastors teach their congregations, and Christian colleges reinforce the message among young people. Unfortunately, several of these links are broken.[2] This chapter provides a picture of what individual Christians ought to expect from the churches, a standard to measure the engagement of their own church on the issues of how they use their stuff and the impact on their eternal soul.

The local church should offer basic Christian education, the mutual support of fellowship, and sermons that touch on practical issues faced in the everyday lives of those in the congregation. With these frequent opportunities for teaching, one would think that people would learn about God and their stuff. But such is rarely the case.

In his book *God and Mammon in America*, Robert Wuthnow suggests, "The doctrines of stewardship hold little meaning for many people. . . . there is a kind of mental or emotional gloss to contemporary religious teaching about money that prevents them from having much impact on how people actually live their lives."[3] In other words, people are coming to church on a weekly basis, soaking up Sunday school lessons and sermons, but not having their view of possessions affected by Christian values. It seems to be the silent subject in most churches. Over the years, churches have chosen to follow the culture rather than act counterculture in this area and speak out boldly under the rule of Christ. Martin Luther warned of selective preaching when he spoke these words: "You can't preach the gospel unless you preach it in light of the issues with which men struggle."

The problem is not that money is never mentioned in churches. Everyone who attends church has had to sit through a message in which budget shortfalls are bewailed. The overriding concern in such cases is getting the immediate needs of the church resolved—completing a building project or maintaining basic financial needs. The problem is that the focus is on guilt to meet church needs, rather than on use of possessions as a way to grow spiritually. Only rarely will a pastor dare speak out on how Christians can make giving an important part of their spiritual lives, and who will talk about money when there is no impending financial crisis.

In light of this typical situation, here are nine reasonable expectations you should have for your local church (whether big or small) to encourage you in your spiritual development through your use of possessions.

i. A Pastoral Staff Trained in Biblical Stewardship and Living It

At the end of his letter to the young pastor Timothy, Paul states what he thinks Timothy ought to be teaching:

> As for those who in the present age are rich,
> command them not to be haughty, or to set their

hopes on the uncertainty of riches, but rather on
God who richly provides us with everything for
our enjoyment. They are to do good, to be rich
in good works, generous, and ready to share.
(1 Timothy 6:17-18, NRSV)

Clearly Paul believed that a young pastor should be
able to speak out on possessions from a biblical stand-
point, and also to challenge his congregation to be willing
to share the money and material things that God has given
them. The pastor has the major responsibility for the
vision, direction, and implementation of stewardship in
the local church.[4]

2. A Written Philosophy of Money and Possessions

Does your church have an articulate vision statement of
stewardship and the use of possessions as a core value of
its ministry? It is commonly thought that about 10 to 30
percent of churches have an active program to teach
about the Christian's relationship with money. An informal phone survey found that most of these churches treat
giving as a membership obligation. In other words, when
an individual (or family) becomes a member of the
church, he or she is expected to contribute to the offerings. The church may have a brief statement to the effect
that members are expected to contribute to the financial
needs of the church, but it is the exception to find a
church with a written statement that encourages giving as
a spiritual discipline.

A good example of the way faith and possessions can
be interwoven is found in the Harvest Community Church
located in Milwaukee, Wisconsin. They distribute a statement on their philosophy of possessions to new members.
This statement sets out both the financial expectations of
the members, as well as the principles by which the
church itself will abide.[5] The following are some excerpts
from this statement:

Primary Source of Church Income
Harvest is dependent on God, through the faithful and generous tithes and offerings of God's people to underwrite the church's ministry, missions, building, and benevolence needs.

Missions Giving
Harvest commits a minimum of 10 percent or more of Sunday offerings to God's work in our world, country, and community. The church has a missions committee and formal guidelines to review all missions requests. Harvest will accept designated missions gifts from individuals in the church that can be passed along to any Christian 501(c)(3) nonprofit organization.

Financial Bible Teaching and Giving Policy
Harvest will teach biblical financial and giving principles through Bible studies, seminars, sermons, etc. . . . The goal of this teaching will be to help people become financially free in their lives, in order to serve and honor God more fully and faithfully.

Fund-raising Events
Because Harvest is dependent on God through the faithful and generous support of God's people, Harvest discourages the use of fund-raising events (banquets, bazaars, carnivals, festivals, bingo . . .) to help meet the church's financial needs.

Quarterly Giving Statements and Financial Information
Harvest will send quarterly giving statements with church financial, missions, benevolence, and/or other financial information and helps to encourage people's faithful and cheerful giving to the Lord's work at Harvest Community Church.

Oversight by CPA
Harvest will have a certified public accountant
involved in overseeing the church's financial policies and procedures.

These points show how a church can deal with financial issues in an elegant and Christlike manner. There is no
attempt to hide the fact that the running of a church
depends on the faithful giving of its members, and it is
clear that members are expected to give to support the
church. But the church presents its own set of values: It
will not use gimmicky tactics to get people to give money;
it has set up a series of checks and balances to ensure
responsible use of these resources; and finally, it promises
to give clear and biblical teaching on the topic (presum-
ably not just during budget emergencies).

If this kind of financial statement were provided by all
churches to their members, and if churches then consistently
abided by their statements, results could be surprising.
Pastors might just find church members becoming more
consistent in their giving, and members might feel more
confident that their church is engaged along with them in
honoring God in financial matters. If your church does not
have such a statement, it may be time to ask for one. It is
imperative that churches have an impeccable process in
place that assumes financial accountability, proper handling
of all areas of finance, and an annual audit process.[6]

This willingness to speak on the financial issues that
surround the Christian life is one of the largest gaps
between New Testament teaching and modern church
practice. Only about 15 percent of pastors feel they have
been adequately equipped by their denomination or seminary to deal with issues relating to possessions. When
asked whether they had instruction in stewardship during
their seminary years, most pastors do not remember more
than one to three hours (not credit hours, but literally one
to three hours!) devoted specifically to stewardship. When
asked if they are comfortable preaching on stewardship,

most will indicate at least a reluctance or discomfort in addressing stewardship more than once a year (generally at budget time). Giving is the least liked topic for a sermon; if church members dread having to hear the "stewardship sermon," the act of giving this sermon is even more dreaded by pastors. This unfortunate reality bodes ill for a mature Christian understanding of the importance of giving for the spiritual life.

3. Money Is Not Treated from a Fund-raising Perspective

When the fiscal year comes to an end and giving is lagging behind, or when an urgent need arises, churches easily slide into fund-raising mode. If dressing up like clowns and juggling offering baskets would cause people to give, many churches would be sorely tempted to try it. And what churches often resort to falls little short of these circus acts. The goal is to get people to dig deeper into their pocketbooks, and no idea is too far out if it will produce this desired end. The alternative to this fund-raising approach is to emphasize giving as part of a Christian's relationship to God.[7]

When the use of money is pursued as a spiritual discipline, the believer is led to ask questions not only about ways he allocates his own money, but also about ways the church uses money. It cannot sit well with someone who practices the spiritual discipline of stewardship to see his church borrowing its main assumptions from modern culture. Part of the individual's stewardship journey includes sincere seeking of discipleship teaching and congregational responsibility in money issues. If money is approached as a spiritual discipline by the corporate body of a church, it becomes part of that church's system of worship, teaching, benevolence considerations, and mission allocations.

Scripture is clear that we are to view giving as a response to the blessings God has given to us. But Scripture also considers giving to be a matter of obedience. Giving is not something that comes easily to most people. People who have developed a lifelong habit of giving often learned to do so through years of discipline and the consistent example of parents or leaders. Such an attitude is not fostered by churches that rely on fund-raising approaches to meet their budget shortfalls or building fund goals. The aim of the church must be to raise Christians who have learned the difficult art of giving, and have also integrated their giving into their entire Christian life. Raising these kinds of Christians takes more time, but in the long run it will build a strong and faithful giving congregation.

4. BIBLICAL GIVING THEMES ARE REGULARLY PREACHED

Since the topics of money and possessions are so prevalent in Scripture, plenty of texts could serve as the basis for sermon material. Christians should expect their pastor to regularly challenge them with these truths. An annual stewardship sermon is better than nothing, but it is not an adequate representation of the rich biblical possibilities. Christians who are not challenged from the pulpit regarding their financial life are spiritually impoverished.

A strong and repeated message from the pulpit that the thoughtful use of money and possessions are part of the Christian life would help to establish positive attitudes and patterns for giving. Such a message would at least partially counteract the 1,700 commercials aired daily that preach consumerism. Stewardship could begin to be incorporated into the overall fabric of the teaching of the church. And when the time comes for the church to make decisions about putting up a new building or adding staff, the congregation would have a set of biblical principles by which to make these decisions.

In the absence of a strong pulpit presence on stewardship, it is little wonder that churches today succumb to cultural pressure. Christians pursue their own natural inclinations in how to use their money and possessions, and continue to escalate their lifestyle at the same rate as people who do not know Christ. Numerous surveys show that the majority of Christians give substantially less than the Old Testament standard of 10 percent of their annual income. It would seem appropriate to point the finger, at least in part, at church pulpits for failing to give American Christians the tools they need to deal successfully with their faith and finances.[8]

Paul speaks of ministers as "servants of Christ and stewards of God's mysteries." One of these divine secrets committed to pastors is the spiritual truth of stewardship. To be a minister of Jesus Christ, a local pastor ought to proclaim what the Bible teaches on stewardship, for "it is required of stewards that they be found trustworthy" (1 Corinthians 4:1-2, NRSV). It has been well stated that "a call to preach is a call to prepare to preach." The minister who feels called to preach on stewardship should also feel the necessity of preparing adequately for the task. Ideally a minister's preparation would include a thorough study of the biblical treatment of stewardship and the kindred subjects of tithing and giving.

Presenting the topic of stewardship from the pulpit is not an easy task. It is hard to broach a subject that connects so personally with the members of the congregation, especially at first. Following are a few points that may help pastors preach stewardship principles more confidently:

Deal with people where they are.
Before preaching a sermon on stewardship, pastors should take time to review the giving patterns of their congregation. Where does the congregation show signs of maturity with use of money and possessions; where do they struggle? Laypeople need practical handles for using their money and good biblical exegesis on what the Bible has to say about stewardship.

Call people to action.
Decisions about how to disperse money to Christian work or whether to begin tithing are easily put off in most North American households. The effective sermon will challenge

people to take action and will provide practical examples of how they can make their resolutions reality. When it comes to money and possessions, pastors cannot sit back and say to themselves, "Let people decide on their own how they will apply these teachings." Human nature being what it is, people will always find a reason to follow a less strenuous route.

Make use of positive role models.

Nothing is more relevant to a person struggling with stewardship questions than to hear how a fellow traveler has wrestled with the same issues and then made strong commitments to God as a result. Pastors ought to make regular use of live testimonies from people in the congregation who have trusted God with their money and how they spend it. These testimonies bring sermons to life and give clear examples about how biblical principles can be applied.

Challenge people.

There is no substitute for the church leadership's own faithful giving. What better example is there than leadership doing what it asks its people to do? Church members may be further encouraged through a stewardship program in which trained leaders visit every home.

5. A LAY COMMITTEE THAT OVERSEES STEWARDSHIP EDUCATION PROGRAMS

Churches often have a finance committee that deals with both spending the money and raising it. This connection between collecting the money and spending it blurs the lines of accountability and keeps the focus of money on a level of fund-raising. The people who decide on budget allocations then must figure out methods to get people to give, and the easiest way to do that is a fund-raising event and a capitulation to culture. Besides this tendency toward fund-raising, the connection between spending and giving falls too easily into standard business models. Businesses generally divide money issues into accounts payable and accounts receivable, and this is indistinguishable from the setup of most churches. All financial decisions are then concentrated in a few people who hold decision-making positions, putting the rest of the congregation in the position of simply paying their membership dues. Such a model takes the spiritual discipline, worship, and growth out of people's giving experience.

A better approach is to have both a stewardship and finance committee. The finance committee is responsible for financial accountability, allocating the resources, managing such necessary items as expenditures, salaries, salary caps, salary reviews, and keeping an eye on how money is coming in and going out. They are responsible for the church's fiscal integrity and keeping it in the black. This committee recognizes that the church budget is also its mission statement. With the budget comes a process that helps members see how they can be part of the action. Every local church has all the resources it needs to accomplish God's vision for their mission. If the resources are not there, either the church has missed God's vision for them or the leaders have failed to help members see how their gifts are needed to advance Christ's mission.

The stewardship committee, on the other hand, is responsible for the integrated programs of stewardship in all areas of the church. Its main job is to watch over how stewardship and money issues will be presented. This group casts the vision and mission. It insists on a faith-based budget process in which no budget is prepared until the gifts of the people are pledged. The committee's decisions are not based on the felt need of the church to support itself, but rather on the need of the people to give to God's work. In essence, the budget is the church vision statement! This lay committee bears the challenge of changing the paradigm of fund-raising style programs to one in which giving is treated as a response of the believer's heart to God's abundant provision. This lay committee would establish continuity through successive classes of elders and deacons, even in the event of the senior pastor's departure. The serving/senior pastor should be part of the stewardship committee and help people see giving as a discipleship issue.

It is also the responsibility of this committee to read the culture and alert members to the seductive ways in which advertising, television, peer pressure, and the like promote a consumer lifestyle and contribute to our society's widespread affluence.

6. AN INTERSOCIAL AND INTEGRATED STEWARDSHIP EDUCATION SYSTEM

The goal for every church is to build a nurturing spiritual community where discussions about stewardship are not perceived as unusual or threatening. Every level of church education ought to be permeated by these values. Messages from the pulpit are laced with references to stewardship; children in primary education are given easy lessons on the importance of giving to God and others; new members are taught the importance of giving in new members' classes. Each major ministry division should be expected to integrate stewardship into its activities. Some suggestions as to how stewardship could be incorporated into each division are shown in chart 8-1, Possible Church Stewardship Emphasis. Achieving this kind of integration will require a number of church committees and departments to work together for planning and strategizing.

Growth as a steward is a process and not limited to one program. Disciples are lifelong learners and thus a church creates opportunities to help members at various life phases understand the stewardship issues they face. Such a program is planned, monitored, and measured to ensure progress. Issues discussed in such an intentional program might include personal financial stewardship, Christian investment, establishing a family budget, saving for college, saving for retirement, and identifying and using spiritual gifts.

Exactly how this integration would be achieved is a question that each individual church must decide for itself.

Chart 8-1

Possible Church Stewardship Emphasis

Ministry Area	Stewardship Integration Action
Adult Education	General stewardship class Budgeting classes Crown Ministries financial classes Mission opportunities classes
Missions	Missions opportunities classes Periodic presentations of needs to the body Periodic updates on accomplishments of mission outreaches

Childhood Education	Each Sunday school class takes responsibility
	    for one mission outreach, donating time
	    and money to that mission
	Children's sermons on giving
	Special envelopes for children, with their name
	    on the envelopes

Small-Group Ministry	Curriculum available for stewardship studies
	Mission representatives available to speak at
	    small-group gatherings
	Encouragement to adopt a family or mission out-
	    reach for the small group

Outreach Ministry	Giving to needy families outside the
	    congregation
	Giving to multiple parachurch ministries
	Sharing stewardship testimonies with other
	    churches, service groups, and teens

Worship Ministry	Use of a stewardship verse at each worship
	    service
	Introduction of the doxology into the worship
	    service
	Periodic sermons about stewardship and using
	    stewardship themes
	Periodic stewardship testimonies as part of the
	    worship service

If a stewardship committee has been established, then this committee may be given at least partial oversight in making sure that stewardship ideas and principles are visible throughout every level of the church.

7. THE USE OF OUTSIDE RESOURCES

Because most churches are inadequately prepared to teach biblical stewardship, they should be ready to draw upon resources available from outside the church. Once stewardship is well entrenched in a church, the presence of outside sources will be less crucial, but for an introduction to stewardship nothing is more effective than bringing in material produced by an organization that specializes in this kind of ministry. Such organizations include *Crown Financial Ministries* [(407) 331-6000, *www.crown.org*] and *Good Sense Ministries*, Willow Creek Association [(847) 765-5000, www.willowcreek.com].

8. TOOLS THAT ENCOURAGE A VARIETY OF WAYS TO GIVE

Nowadays people hold many assets other than cash. In a few years, passing the offering plate may seem a quaint reminder of bygone days.[9] Churches should strive to make giving as easy and practical as possible for members. Some options for convenient giving might include the following:

- Open a charity account in the church's name at a local brokerage firm. Usually free of charge, these accounts provide a convenient mechanism for giving appreciated stocks and other investments.
- Provide planned giving services that encourage people to give annuities, set up trusts, or include the church in their will. It is estimated that trillions of dollars will be passed down in the next ten to twenty years, so the church should be encouraging members to give beyond their own lifetimes. Helping members establish a personal foundation is another avenue to consider.

- Provide information about ministries the church supports. No longer can we count on loyalty alone to ensure that people will give. Church members need clear teaching and mechanisms for giving that fit their circumstances. The methodology for giving must match people's different lifetime passages.
- Pursue convenience mechanisms such as payroll deductions, automatic electronic fund transfers, and options for giving via a Web site.

In choosing these new tools for their congregations, churches should take care that they do not contradict their own stewardship teachings. For example, what kind of message would be sent to the congregation if a church taught that debt should be avoided, but then encouraged people to give to the building fund through their credit cards? Or what would be the message if a church spoke out against materialism, but at the same time asked the day traders in the congregation if they would like to contribute from their stocks?

9. REGULAR COMMUNICATION ABOUT THE CHURCH'S FINANCIAL POSITION

If a church's leadership expects members to exemplify biblical stewardship, it is crucial that the church itself be run on the same open and clear principles. The best way to make it evident that the church is being run on such principles is to establish regular patterns of communication with the congregation. Financial information should not only be released once a year at the annual business meeting, but should be available at all times. And since a church expects its members to give 10 percent of their income to Christian work, it is natural that the church should make some similar sacrifices by giving to various missions organizations or outreach programs. The church should work within the general principle that, everything it asks the individual member to do, it will do as well.

But no matter how scrupulous a church's leadership is

about its financial accounts, it will do no good unless this is communicated to the members. There are many ways to accomplish this, but following are a few that have proven successful:

- Send periodic giving statements to people to encourage them to be more faithful in their giving. The main purpose of the statement is to provide people with an update of their giving to date, and to help keep them from getting too far behind. Furthermore, it challenges them to consider their giving as it relates to the faithfulness to God. One covenant church began sending out monthly statements with a letter from a church board member describing his excitement about what God was doing in the church. They saw an immediate 11 percent increase in giving.
- Send out faith-and-possessions newsletters that contain testimonies of people in the congregation who have learned to give as an act of faith and grace. This newsletter should also focus on the accomplishments of the church made possible through the faithful giving of the members.
- Provide ongoing stewardship thoughts in all venues of church communication. An example of this might be to include a weekly stewardship verse in the bulletin, or a short stewardship lesson from the pastor in the monthly newsletter.

These nine points, taken together, will provide a church with the foundation for a solid stewardship ministry that is a process, not a program, and is intentional, not spontaneous. Although real change in financial habits is a long-term effort, it won't happen if church leadership never bothers to start.

CHAPTER NINE

What Families and Educators Should Be Doing

A child is a person who is going to carry on what you started. A child is going to sit where you're sitting, and when you're gone, attend to those things which you think are important. You may adopt all the policies you please, but how they'll be carried out depends on that child. He or she will assume control of your cities, states, and nations. Is going to move in and take over your churches, schools, universities, and corporations. All your books are going to be judged, praised, or condemned by that child. The fate of humanity is in his or her hands. Teach them well!

—ABRAHAM LINCOLN

WE LIVE IN A CONSUMER-DOMINATED CULTURE THAT WORSHIPS stuff. We also live at a time when Christian institutions are relatively silent on the subject of our use of possessions and spiritual growth. Within the context of this difficult environment, there are three institutions that we should hold accountable to assist us in our Christian stewardship walk: (1) the church, (2) the family, and (3) Christian colleges and seminaries. Chapter 8 outlined expectations for the church; this chapter will bring into focus the education role of the family, Christian colleges, and seminaries—for only as our methods of education succeed will the roots of stewardship be revitalized.

Assuming that the purpose of our Christian institutions is to develop mature disciples of Christ, with God's Word at the center, it would seem natural to focus on biblical stewardship. Ideally, positive teaching on the use of possessions would reinforce the concept that the primary purpose of Christian giving is learning to put God first in every area of life.

Unfortunately this Christian educational stewardship chain is broken! As mentioned in the last chapter, seminaries are admittedly reluctant to teach biblical stewardship, and expose their graduates to as little as three hours of teaching on the subject. Christian colleges and universities are similarly silent. And thus it is no surprise that most pastors are loath to touch upon financial issues from the pulpit. They simply do not have the necessary training—biblical and practical—to speak authoritatively on the topic. As a result, the family is often ill-equipped on this subject as well.

Jeavons and Basinger point out that with the void of positive discussions on money in churches, colleges, seminaries, and among families, one of the few sources of education in this regard is the people asking for money.[1] However, this group has been most concerned with the bottom line of what works, not the spiritual state of the potential giver.

And so, into this space abdicated by teachings of our churches, schools, and families, our culture's materialistic values (broadcast on TV, radio, and in the malls) flow freely into the minds of our children.

For a change to take place, it is essential that individual believers who have learned the spiritual benefits of a strong commitment to Christian stewardship raise the expectations for the Christian institutions that they associate with, starting with their own family. There is much room for improvement; and you can be instrumental in encouraging that change. The purpose of this chapter is to provide an overview of what the individual Christian ought to expect from these institutions, since they are the places influencing the spiritual leaders of tomorrow. Against this backdrop, you can measure your own family and Christian schools with which you are familiar, then ask questions about how each can better follow Christ's teaching and the role you can play in making that happen.

THE FAMILY

While books, magazines, radio programs, and other materials about the Christian family abound, resources to instruct the family in the use of their possessions is limited. Developed here are four suggestions that will help a family: (1) model stewardship values, (2) demonstrate that money comes from working, (3) create a lifestyle that encourages giving, and (4) practice giving as a habit. These principles can play themselves out in many different ways in a family's life, but they are all critical when wrapped around the proper motive and knowledge that all belongs to God.

MODEL STEWARDSHIP VALUES

From birth, our natural human sin nature is to be self-centered, to see the world as rotating around ourselves, and to want things for ourselves. It is as typical for a child not to want to share as it is to say "Gimme." When you look at newsstands, the predominant titles seem to focus on "What's in it for me?" or how to have this or that next pleasure or experience. Left to ourselves, we are natural-born builders of our own kingdoms here on the earth.

While it is a big help to have a supportive church, the best place for educating scriptural truths on stewardship is in the home. It is here that children will not only hear the right words, but see the right actions and experience the attitudes that counter our consumer culture and the self-centeredness into which we were all born. One reason for this is reflected in the oft-quoted saying of Albert Schweitzer: "There are three ways to teach a child. The first is example, the second is by example, and the third is by example."

As was affirmed in chapter 1, God is watching our every move. So too are our children. They are able to see by example what we truly value. If we say that our possessions are a tool for furthering God's kingdom, a trademark of who is Lord of our life, and a test to see our soul's place in heaven, then it should be self-evident to them.

Ephesians 6:12 informs Christians that they are engaged in a great battle that also requires great resources. If we spend resources on our own individual desires, it prevents their use for building God's kingdom. We need to ask ourselves if all that we do strategically maximizes resources for God's use.[2]

It all comes back to lifestyle choices. For example, how a family celebrates Christmas—with a materialistic focus or a thankful heart focus—tells a lot about which kingdom they are following. The type of vacations you take, the expense of the car you drive, all testify to what kingdom you are building. Do you live within your means? Do you try to repair things for much less than the cost of buying new? When you make giving decisions, do you include the children? All such choices are under their thoughtful gaze and are of significant influence on their lives.

YOU GET MONEY FROM WORKING

While this may seem obvious and trite to some, actually it is a very important principle. We live in an age of lotteries, million-dollar television game show winnings, instant cash, and an apparently endless amount of material goods. With so many ways of seemingly gaining money without working, it is important to teach children that the way life works is that you are paid for your efforts. Possessions don't just happen.[3]

In the family, then, no matter the child's age, it is important to find age-relevant jobs (yard work, housework) that allow him to earn an allowance so he can in turn save and give it back. For instance, my boys were responsible for the lawn and they knew that they didn't get an allowance until they completed the work.

As a parent, your expectations for each child should be very clear. Often a checklist on the refrigerator is a good system to keep everyone communicating on expectations and progress. Whatever the system, the key issue is to teach by example that money comes from working.

CREATE A LIFESTYLE THAT ENCOURAGES GIVING

Not spending more than you earn and promoting saving so you can give back to God is a lifestyle that creates discipline in both parents and children. It is this habit of saving that leads to the attitude of a mature steward.

One of the greatest financial pitfalls of our time is the notion that the way you make ends meet is to earn more. Actually, the way to live within your means and to leverage more of your assets toward giving is to learn to live off less. This starts by giving and saving off the top of your income.

Many systems exist to encourage a disciplined lifestyle for children. An example of one system is that of the Bander family.[4] This family has three children ranging from ages eight to fourteen. For many years, they have paid their children an allowance for the assigned weekly chores. Their method of payment is quite interesting — always with single dollar bills and loose change. On top of the Banders' counter are nine glass jars—three jars per child—and a calculator. Each jar bears a label: church, missions, personal. As the children receive their allowance, they must calculate how much to place in each jar. For the Bander family, 15 percent goes in the church jar, 10 percent in the missions jar, and the rest gets placed in the personal jar. The $1 bills and change makes it easy to divide the money between the jars.

The Banders believe that "the 10 percent tithe is a starting point—a bare minimum of what one should give." They believe that by teaching their kids early that all they have belongs to God, they are not "confined to a specific percentage." "We want our kids to understand that it's not 10 percent God's, 90 percent theirs," says Mrs. Bander.

The Bander children have no complaints about sharing their allowance with God. In fact, their parents state that more times than not, the children become aware of a need within the body of Christ and oftentimes rob their "personal" jar to help those in need. As Mrs. Bander states, "When you see a child put someone else's needs first and share their own money, you know their heart has been changed."

Another way to approach the jar system is for the child to save 10 percent, give 10 percent, and keep the balance. Whatever methods you use, be sure to involve the children in the family giving.

GIVING IS A HABIT

Probably one of the easiest things in life to procrastinate about is giving. It is so easy to say, "I never know when I'll need that money." In so doing, we insult God and His ability to provide for all our needs.

What better place to teach our children the habit of giving than in the home? To encourage them to save, to live as inexpensively as possible, and to include them in the giving decisions is a tremendous opportunity to train up mature stewards.

Here is a story of how one young family involved their four children in the giving process:

> I remember the evening we sat around the kitchen table with the kids for a family meeting. The older ones had a general idea of how much money we made. We talked about the material things we could run out and buy and discussed the difference between investing in things that are temporal versus eternal. I remember my eight-year-old son saying that it would be silly to spend all that money on ourselves when it could be used to help those with *real* needs.
>
> We presented to the kids the list of ministry opportunities we were aware of. It was fun to see their eyes light up when they understood that our gifts would have an impact around the world. Our meeting concluded by pulling out the checkbook and then praying for each ministry or person individually. It was one of the most moving

experiences we have ever had as a family.

We are a changed family as a result of these experiences. We understand now more than ever that we are responsible to manage the monies God entrusts to us. We now realize that all we have belongs to Him, not a certain percentage confined to certain times of the year. Our priorities have changed dramatically. We don't look at future income as building a "war chest" to serve our own needs or to fund our retirement. We want our business and our lives to be the vehicle through which God distributes His resources to His people. When we think about the lives our gifts have touched, we are overwhelmed to think that God used *us* to help accomplish His work.[5]

It is experiences like this that will develop solid stewardship values for the future among our children and at the same time provide a reason for parents to be faithful stewards.

WHAT YOU SHOULD EXPECT FROM A CHRISTIAN COLLEGE OR UNIVERSITY

After the family and church, the next most important institutions for passing along stewardship truth are Christian colleges and seminaries. Following are ten expectations you should have from colleges and three additional responsibilities of seminaries.

1. Written Statement in School's Catalog

Christian colleges, universities, and seminaries generally publish statements in their catalogs that elaborate their worldviews and the objectives of their educational program. If a school is serious about stewardship, it is important that these values are expressed and then noted how they are worked out in the curriculum. If stewardship does not rank high enough in importance to find a place in this statement, it is highly unlikely that these principles will find any space in the school's teaching either. This statement on stewardship ought to outline the importance Christ placed on teaching about possessions and cover five primary themes:

- God has provided all our resources.
- God has given Christians the responsibility to manage these resources.
- How we use our possessions has an impact on our eternal soul.
- God will ultimately hold us responsible for how we use His resources.
- Believers are to be cheerful and charitably minded givers.

The school that chooses to highlight these points in its statement of educational philosophy and Christian worldview will have a starting foundation for implementing them into the active life of the student body and faculty.

2. A Written Theology of Possessions and the Importance of Stewardship in Spiritual Development

Since a vital link exists between faith and possessions, it is essential that Christian institutions have a biblical statement laying out where they stand in this crucial aspect of Christian experience. This can be thought of as an expanded and more technical version of the short statement provided in the catalog. If such a statement does not exist, a starting point could be to pull together a group of like-minded people (perhaps those interested in spiritual formation on campus) to draft and circulate one.[6]

3. Faculty and Staff Are Provided Training in Stewardship

Because of the general lack of training about possessions in churches, seminaries, and homes, influential people on campus must be taught stewardship principles if they are to convey these truths to Christian young people. Once a theology of stewardship is developed, this training can be done in a special seminar, led either by a staff member or someone from an organization such as Crown Financial Ministries. If stewardship is not modeled by the school's leadership, there is no reason to think that students will adopt a stewardship lifestyle.

4. Campus Personnel Are Provided Opportunities to Share How They Incorporate Stewardship into Their Lives

Mentoring and modeling are a vital part of the education process, so it is important to introduce opportunities in which the school's leadership can demonstrate how stewardship and the giving lifestyle has changed their lives. One possibility for accomplishing this would be brown-bag lunches featuring members of the faculty discussing their personal experiences. Discussion groups or chapel presentations are other viable venues.

5. Faculty Are Encouraged to Integrate Biblical Stewardship Principles into Their Classes

At the core of Christian colleges and seminaries is the belief that the Christian worldview influences every academic discipline, indeed every aspect of life. These Christian institutions strive to integrate faith and learning. However, biblical stewardship principles have gotten lost in the integration process. This takes effort—it may even be necessary at first to create a committee in charge of overseeing this process. But the end result of a student body well trained in stewardship values is worth the effort to all of Christendom.[7]

6. Chapel Presentations Address the Spiritual Aspects of Our Use of Money and Possessions

In many Christian colleges, universities, and seminaries, spiritual truth is transmitted during formal chapel times. Those in charge of programming these events should intentionally include speakers and forums that address and model the topic of biblical stewardship and related themes. Especially on the seminary level, this kind of training would be invaluable to the wider church as it would mold future pastors in this area, then send them forth to model these truths in their churches. Just as in a church setting, public testimonies about the spiritual benefits of stewardship are an effective way to communicate to students.

7. Students Are Provided Extracurricular Opportunities that Encourage a Life of Stewardship

Most Christian colleges talk openly about being concerned for the whole person, which is why they are predominantly residence colleges. This environment provides excellent teaching opportunities for dealing with possessions and money. Informal discussions (or structured talks) very often lead to meaningful interaction about such basics as debt, money management, and credit cards. A good place to start this emphasis is with new student orientation—which, incidentally, is when students typically sign up for their first credit card and their money-management challenges begin.

8. Parachurch Organizations Specializing in Stewardship Are Encouraged to Offer Their Programs on Campus

The stewardship-friendly campus is so actively concerned about this matter that it encourages specialized groups to come on campus to train students in stewardship principles. The administration should encourage small-group workshops led by parachurch organizations that specialize in biblical stewardship topics. Through these small groups, students could be instructed on a personal and professional level, and in the process get to know resources that they could one day introduce to their own congregation. Crown Financial Ministries has small-group workshops designed specifically for the college-age student [(770) 534-1000, *www.crown.org*]. Also, MMA provides a stewardship university program and online instruction [(800) 348-7468, *www.GivingProject.net, www.StewardshipUniversity.org, www.MMA-online.org]*.

9. Spiritual Formation Curriculum

Besides encouraging an emphasis in biblical stewardship across the curriculum, a specific class elective also could be made available. Special course work on spiritual formation is popular these days, and incorporating stewardship into such classes would be an ideal way to teach this important topic.

10. Institutional Business and Fund-raising Practices Are Consistent with Biblical Principles

A college or seminary is obviously sending out mixed messages if it teaches one thing when it comes to money, but practices another. As with a church, it behooves the college or seminary to be open with students and faculty about its financial position. Why is the college raising tuition? Why is a fancier, more expensive vendor being hired to feed students in the cafeteria? Why is the college borrowing money to build a new facility? If these kinds of issues are dealt with openly, then students will be more encouraged to look closely at their own financial practices.

Fund-raising practices (also discussed in chapter 7) are another area in which colleges can often be tempted to go against biblical principles in favor of raising more money for that next project. It is crucial that the leadership of a college pays careful attention to the methods it uses to raise money; because like it or not, these actions model values to students, parents, and others. The full-orbed biblical stewardship program of a Christian college or university will assure that the institution's fund-raising efforts are consistent with its principles. Fund-raising should not induce guilt, and it should place the spiritual importance of giving above the immediate need of the university to raise a certain number of dollars.

ADDITIONAL EXPECTATIONS OF SEMINARIES

While each of the preceding points applies to seminaries as well, because of the obvious focus of seminary education to train pastors, certain additional areas apply. These include the following:

1. A Full Complement of Courses Offered on Biblical Stewardship

The intentional seminary curriculum, built on mature theology, ought to provide a cadre of courses on biblical stewardship that are integrated into its course offerings. Stewardship has applications in many areas of study, and it would be most pertinent in spiritual formation and hermeneutics.

2. Mentoring Opportunities Provided

The seminary that takes seriously its obligation to students in matters of stewardship will provide real-life mentoring opportunities under the guidance of gifted mentors. These experiences with mature Christian teachers would build leaders who have a heart to lead their congregations to spiritual maturity.

3. Local Pastors Are Given Training Opportunities at the Seminary

Because pastors often are inadequately trained in stewardship issues, it is a great opportunity of outreach for seminaries to provide classes, seminars, and special discussions on the care and feeding of the flock with regard to money.

YOUR ENCOURAGEMENT CAN HELP

We have now looked at what we might reasonably expect from our families, Christian colleges, universities, and seminaries in regard to helping us grow spiritually through the use of our possessions. The Christian who has felt his or her life transformed by the power of stewardship principles, and has learned the vital link between spiritual growth and giving, will inevitably be disappointed with the state of these important Christian institutions. And so these points are not envisioned as a checklist that institutions must pass if they are to have support, but rather as a set of guidelines we all should be urging them to accomplish. As Christians come to resemble the materialism of the surrounding culture, sadly there will be fewer willing to speak out for change. If this is an area that concerns you, contact colleges and seminaries you care about, expressing your desire that they acknowledge the importance of biblical stewardship and commit to teaching it. As a result of these efforts, change for the good will happen, building up the souls of the saints.

CHAPTER TEN

Keeping Your Soul Alive

One more revival—only one more—is needed, the revival of Christian stewardship, the consecration of the money power to God. When the revival comes, the Kingdom of God will come in a day.

—HORACE BUSHNELL

IMAGINE WITH ME, ONE DAY YOU COME HOME AND START LEAFING through your mail, sorting the personal letters from the bills and the appeals, when your eye catches an envelope teaser that says, "Give No More." Intrigued, you open this appeal to find a brief letter stating, "All our needs are met, so please give no more."

A short while later, the phone rings (while you're eating dinner, of course), and it's a familiar ministry that you consistently give to each time they call. Instead of the usual script—obviously read word for word—the caller says, "I've called to say thanks for all you've given. We have more than enough, so please, please, 'Give no more.'"

If you're like me, you're probably saying, "No way—that could never happen." Well, it happened to the people of Israel, as recorded in Exodus 36:6-7. Moses went even one step further. Not only were the Israelites instructed to give no more, but they "were restrained from bringing more, because what they already had was more than enough to do all the work." It seems that when God's people became faithful, generous givers, the needs took care of themselves.

Is this just an Old Testament myth? Is it possible today?

Consider 2 Corinthians 9:12 (NASB), where God makes the promise of "fully supplying the needs of the saints," to meet and exceed all needs of the church worldwide. When God's people give according to God's plan of stewardship, the needs will be met, and people will be told to "give no more."

Again, you might say, "Let's get real—maybe in the Bible, but not today." Yet if this were the giving pattern today, I fully believe God would tell us, "Well done, faithful Christians. You have shown true stewardship. Give no more." This is one reason God spends so much time on the topic of possessions in Scripture. He understands its importance and the power it has in our lives and upon His kingdom. As emphasized throughout the book, our possessions are a powerful tool for good or evil, the key to the growth of our soul, and the trademark of our lives to those around us.

If individual Christians were to turn the tide and grow stewardship roots grounded in God's Word, the impact on His work through the church would be immense and the transformation of lives would be profound. The focus of this chapter is: (1) to consider the impact to the church, the individual, and society as a whole if these roots were to become vital; and (2) to suggest ways that this revitalization of our stewardship could take place.

WHAT DIFFERENCE WOULD IT MAKE?

A few years back at a denominational general conference, the proposed budget for the ministry greatly exceeded income, and a hot debate ensued. After awhile, an accountant stood up to say he had done some figuring: "If all the members of the denomination went on welfare and tithed their monthly welfare check, the income of the ministry would increase 700 percent!"

Just imagine what could be accomplished if Christians began to tithe with their much larger incomes! The church's full adoption of Christian stewardship principles would literally transform our culture. Here are some of the possibilities:

- The poor would be cared for.
- People would be satisfied because their souls would be in a right relationship with God.
- Givers would not feel pressured; they would have the freedom to be themselves and grow spiritually through their giving.
- Givers would be blessed.
- Fund-raisers would not feel like manipulation.
- The amount of giving to religion alone would increase from 1 to 10 percent or more, from about $90 billion to $210 billion.

Another way to look at the potential impact is presented in Russell Chandler's book *Racing Toward 2001: The Forces Shaping America's Religious Future*. He states: "If church members were to boost their giving to an average of 10 percent of their income (the tithe), the additional funds could eliminate the worst of world poverty . . . plus another $17 billion for domestic need—all while maintaining church activities at current levels."[1]

This sounds great in theory, but the reality is that giving by church members is far below 10 percent: Roman Catholics average about 1.5 percent; mainline Protestants 2.8 percent; Evangelicals about 4.8 percent; and the general population less than 1 percent. Even so, research on giving demonstrates how consistently strong American religious giving has been. Consider the following points: (1) America is the most generous nation in the world, giving more than $203 billion in the year 2000; (2) the American giving tradition is religious in its philanthropic as well as its charitable dimension;[2] (3) religion receives, by far, more money than any other constituency;[3] (4) giving and volunteering are dominated by those most actively involved in organized religion (73 percent of all contributions given to charities other than religion come from the group that supports religion and claims religious membership and involvement);[4] (5) there is a strong correlation between fervency of faith and giving/volunteering (the

most important indicator of who gives in America is fre-
quency of church attendance, Bible study, and prayer);[5]
and (6) the absence of compelling Judeo-Christian religious inclinations operates as a major factor to explain the
lack of giving among non-donors.[6]

Evangelical Christians provide a historical taproot for
much of America's giving strength and provide a huge portion of the energy that powers the locomotive of the entire
$203 billion giving train. Evangelical Christians constitute
the largest and most active component of religious life in
North America (almost one-third of the nation's population), and a much higher percentage of them practice their
faith actively than either of the two other major faith
groups — Catholics or mainline Protestants. Evangelicals
give as a percentage of their income about two times more
than mainline Protestants (4.79 percent versus 2.84 percent),[7] almost three times more than Roman Catholics,[8] and
at least four times more than the general population.
Indeed, 80 percent of all adults who give 10 percent or
more of their income are born-again Christians.[9] It seems
self-evident, if giving is going to change, we evangelicals
will need to lead the way by making the spiritual connection between our soul and our possessions.

HOW DO WE REVITALIZE OUR STEWARDSHIP ROOTS?

How can we find direction again, reconnecting our earthly
possessions and our eternal soul? More importantly, how
can we revitalize our stewardship roots to the extent that
we respond to human need without discrimination, make
sacrifices for others without concern for personal benefit,
and ultimately give glory to God? Let me illustrate with a
story from the sports world.

Football has been a big part of my life, teaching me
many lessons. I played high school ball, as did my two
sons. My oldest, Brian, went on and was captain and all-
conference player for a major Division 1 collegiate program. One lesson you learn in football is that when you
lose, the practices are quite different from when you win.

Legendary Green Bay Packers coach Vince Lombardi once suffered a humiliating road loss to the archrival Chicago Bears. Outraged at his team's poor performance, he had the players get into their cold, sweaty, and bloodied uniforms immediately upon their return to Green Bay. Then he had the stadium lights turned on and sat the team down in the middle of Lambeau Field. Staring at the faces of defeated athletic humanity, he said to them with insulting words: "This is a football. Today we go back to the basics—blocking, tackling, passing, running, and catching. This is a football. We're going back to the basics."

Lombardi was telling this to grown men, some of them veterans with fifteen to twenty years of experience. They knew the playbook better than anything else in their life. It's like saying to the conductor of the New York Philharmonic, "Maestro, this is a whole note." Or to a head librarian, "This is a book." Or to a mother of four small children, "This is a bottle." Exactly how basic do you have to get? In Lombardi's opinion—very basic. He believed that to win in football, you perfect the basics.

Similarly with God and our stuff: This is God's world, this is God's money, we are God's people. The place to begin is at the foundation of our life of faith and soul development. Drawing from David McKenna's "Giving Is Not Guaranteed,"[10] here are ten back-to-basics steps to help us get stewardship in its proper perspective and to focus on the soul concerns of God's kingdom.

1. Acknowledge Our God-Given Role as Stewards

The roots have been withered, as explained earlier, from the erosion of the soil surrounding them, so when we talk about the basics of revitalizing Christian stewardship, we are talking about more than a box of Miracle Grow or a shot of B-12!

Christians need to begin with a whole different world-view—a whole new set of values. Our culture says, "You are in control," "You can do it," and "Just do it!" We have to acknowledge that God is the One in control and the job description He has given us is that of stewards. We must realize that we are created by God, in His image, with the purpose of serving Him—not ourselves. We have value because of God, and as Christians we are in an eternal covenant relationship between God and the earth. All that we do is to be done as unto the Lord. We are not people of this world who can adopt ethical systems or popular practices because they work. Finally, our resources are not our own, for God is the true owner of everything.

With this biblical perspective, giving opportunities become ways to demonstrate good stewardship and distribute what God has given. The role of those asking for funds is not to manipulate, but to present opportunities and to educate a person toward a proper relationship to God. If God fired people for bad stewardship, the unemployment lines would be very long! Would you be in one?

2. Define Stewardship Values Personally and Reorganize Priorities

Once we have acknowledged the fact that we were created to fulfill a stewardship role, we need to personally define stewardship, then reorganize our priorities. Stewardship is God's way of raising people—not man's way of raising money. God is working in us to help us become the people He wants us to be through how we learn to give.

The Reluctant Steward, a study on stewardship and development funded by The Lilly Endowment, concluded that we must look "first and foremost to a renewed understanding of the theology and practice of Christian stewardship."[11] And as individuals we must make this a personal quest to realize within ourselves the meaning of being a good steward.

A theology of stewardship needs to be understood in the broadest terms if it is to have the power to change lives. The steward has some power, but recognizes that that power is delegated—by God. And ultimately, the steward acknowledges that this attitude must impact every aspect of daily life, including: our environment, bodies, relationships, time, talents, and treasures. What other response is there to our wonderful redemption?

3. Live Vertically in a Chaotic Horizontal World

Once we acknowledge and define our role, then we need to live it out. Christians are called to be "in the world but not of the world." I think of an astronaut walking in space—weightless in an alien environment connected to support systems only by an umbilical cord that attaches to their space suit and provides oxygen and the proper pressure to keep the body together. That is a picture of how we should live—in the world, but connected and dependent on God as our lifeline.

Christians have become "resident aliens" as Stanley Hauerwas and William Willimon explain in their book by this title. The question Hauerwas and Willimon ask is this:

> What does it mean for us to live in a culture of unbelief, a culture that does not even know it does not believe because it still lives on the residue of Christian civilization? What does it mean for the pastor to have for a job description not the sustenance of a service club within a generally Christian culture, but the survival of a colony within an alien society?[12]

As we think of the loss of "cultural authority," described by Os Guinness, that leaves our culture without norms, or as we remember the "culture wars," explained by James Hunter,[13] that leave Christians without a united, cohesive approach, we realize that the Christian community is compromised in its approach to our times. In our stewardship role we need to acknowledge the need, define our position, and start acting upon our values by living vertically in a chaotic horizontal world.

4. Pray for Spiritual Revival

As Waldo Werning reminds us in *Supply-Side Stewardship,* "Stewardship is a life style, a process, not a program. The life style is dictated to us by God, that we may become functioning members of the body of Christ in the world. We are not just like the Body: We are the Body."[14] History tells us that concerns for stewardship issues heightened after the Reformation and after the two Great Awakenings at the end of the last two centuries. If the roots of Christian stewardship are going to be revitalized, it will start with a spiritual revival. Likewise, Christians coming to terms with their stewardship responsibilities will grow spiritually as they get themselves into a correct relationship with God and His creation.

Princeton sociologist Robert Wuthnow discussed his three-year research project of religion and economic values in *The Christian Century,* and concluded the following: "Faith makes little difference to the ways in which people actually conduct their financial affairs."[15] Ultimately stewardship is a spiritual issue of people getting right with the Lord. Our prayers need to focus on three concerns:

- Redemption of the individual
- Revival in the church
- Awakening in the culture

Thin soil cannot sustain tall growth. We must deepen and enrich the soil so our biblical stewardship roots can grow deep. We need spiritual renewal for ourselves, our churches, and our culture. Let us faithfully pray to this end.

5. Facilitate Christian Stewardship Education

James Davidson Hunter says that in the midst of the culture war, the educational institution is the "central institution through which the larger social order is reproduced."[16] What applies to society applies especially to the church and its educational institutions.

Regrettably, as the notion of stewardship has withered,

so has teaching about it. We must challenge our churches, seminaries, and Christian schools to get stewardship back in the curriculum and into the heads and hearts of the people.

6. Promote Stewardship-Motivated Giving and Asking

In general, both the Christian givers and the Christian askers are ignoring the basic premises of stewardship, and creating a catch-22 situation in the process—who is responsible and who is going to act first? According to George Barna's extensive research, the large, emerging generations of "boomers and busters are more inclined to give to organizations whose purpose is to serve humankind than those whose purpose is to serve God."[17] If correct, this attitude is straight out of the secularized philanthropic/development mind-set of our culture!

In the pressure to meet bottom-line needs, Christian fund-raisers have by-and-large adopted the values of the world. They stress benefits to the giver, provide premiums, and try to be as emotional as possible. Christian givers go right along with this secular pitch, and thereby lose spiritual sensitivity in their lives. Many feel obligated to give to every appeal. Where is the work of the Spirit in all of this?

Think what would happen if people wrote to organizations, revolting against their manipulative methods? Someone has to stop the cycle. Are you willing to step out and be a leader? What nonprofit CEO is willing to risk initially less income to get his or her organization in line with Scripture? What fund-raiser is willing to change the fund-raising approach to encourage ministry and stewardship-motivated giving? The process must start somewhere.

7. Resist Self-interest

In his book *Habits of the Heart*, Robert Bellah traces the influence of self-interest in the shaping of American character where we "do what we want to do for our own profit" and "be what we want to be for our own pleasure."[18] In his sequel, *The Good Society*, Bellah traces the radical self-interest to the primary institutions of the culture. By definition, these institutions are intended to mediate between self-interest and the common good. Rather, says Bellah, our homes, churches, and schools have become "arenas of hostility of competing self-interest rather than nurturing communities for the common good. Subtle self-interest is no respecter of persons or institutions."[19]

A big part of the problem is that givers and askers place a higher value on culturally instilled self-interest than on following God's stewardship principles. For the giver, this self-interest is demonstrated in desire for personal benefits, control of the way the money is used, and attempts to control the organization itself.

Recently, a group of twelve Christian CEOs and fundraisers met to discuss current trends in their organizations. They concluded self-interest is a significant trait of their donors, who are asking, "What's in it for me?" and becoming mistrustful of ministries. On the other side, those asking for funds are feeling more pressure. Add to that a proliferation of ministries, greater resistance to giving, and less loyalty among donors, compounded by the troubled economy and personal debt.

Putting self first is an issue of sin. Have you ever thought about the lack of stewardship as a sin? Are you willing to change your self-interested ways and follow God's way instead?

8. Facilitate Leadership Who Understand Biblical Stewardship

The materialism current away from biblical generosity and concern for the soul is so strong in our culture that Christian leadership must make every possible effort to reverse the tide. Max DePree gives Christian leaders this advice in *Leadership Is an Art*: "The first responsibility of a leader is to define reality. The last is to say thank you. In between the two, the leader must become a servant and a debtor."[20]

Our church, school, seminaries, and home leadership are avoiding stewardship issues. Where are the servant leaders who are willing to take a stand, define reality, and make a difference?

I think of the Garden of the Gods, magnificent red-rock spires on the edge of Colorado Springs that attract visitors from around the world. Actually the rock formations are the result of centuries of erosion, and the standing spires remain because of an inner core of solid rock and a cap of granite on top. We need leaders (like Daniel in the Old Testament) with that same inner core of integrity to stand on top of their profession and proclaim the truths of stewardship.

9. Encourage Research/Writing/Sermons

The field of Christian stewardship is relatively unexplored—particularly by Christians. We must encourage research and writing to explore its individual and institutional implications. Probably the greatest theologian of our time is Carl F. H. Henry, who has written practically a library full of books. A constant theme of his writing is that we desperately need Christian researchers and writers to confront the pagan philosophies of our day. If Christian stewardship is to resume its place among believers and impact our culture accordingly, there must be a concerted effort to research, write, and speak with authority, to confront the secular ideas of our time, and to proclaim the stewardship truth to our generation and the generations to come.

10. Disciple Others

Most of us see giving as an obligation supported by law, guilt, and judgment. When it comes to our stewardship of God's creation, we fail to put our thankfulness into practice, let alone help disciple others. When God gave us the physical environment, He created it and then pronounced it "very good." He then entrusted us not just to have "dominion" over the earth, but to "tame and tend" it and all things in it (Genesis 2, KJV). The Israelites are a perfect example of this commandment, for though God gave the land of promise for their use, the title remained in His name.

It is so very easy to excuse how we use, spend, and give our money. The challenge is great, but the potential for good even greater. Are you willing to do your part?

WHAT WILL SHAPE THE FUTURE?

Most futurists do not predict the future. They make their fortune by interpreting the present in a new way. While only God truly knows the future, the strong cultural and religious shifts we are experiencing today are paving the way for a much different future than we have ever experienced. Who would ever imagine how terrorism in the United States would affect our lives and that the Red Cross would at one time say "give no more"?

Past evidence indicates that a spiritual awakening and renewal in our culture will transform our materialistic greed into the most elementary principles of biblical stewardship, which are at the heart of generous giving. In the 1740s and 1750s, revitalization to biblical stewardship came through the spiritual renewal of the first Great Awakening under the ministries of Jonathan Edwards and George Whitefield. It would appear that the future of our giving from a Christian stewardship motive depends more and more upon a Great Awakening in our day.

We need to hear historian Timothy Smith in his classic work, *Revivalism and Social Reform*, explain again how God came near to renew the roots of biblical stewardship over one hundred years ago. It was not because entrepreneurs and economists read Darwin's book, *On the Descent of Man*. Rather, Smith says, "It was . . . due to the fact that in countless revivals the 'tongue of fire' had descended upon the disciples, freeing them from the bondage of sin and selfishness, and dedicating them to the task of making over the world."[21]

An awakening in the twenty-first century has the potential to make us realize that: (1) God has provided all our resources; (2) He has given us the responsibility to manage those resources as stewards; (3) We can choose to experience the joy of being generous; and (4) He will ultimately hold us accountable for how we use His resources. Such a realization could do no other than cause giving to escalate. Are you actively praying to this end?

There are some encouraging signs in recent years that indicate a movement toward focusing on the link between earthly possessions and our eternal soul. The efforts of Crown Financial Ministries, the Mennonite Giving Project, the Christian Stewardship Association, the Generous Giving Project, and the Kingdom Seekers, to name a few, are awakening believers to these areas of God's truth.

In his 1985 book *The Steward, a Biblical Symbol Come of Age,* Douglas John Hall states: "It seems to me [Christian stewardship] is a precious gem whose time has come."[22] This vision starts with committed Christians like you and me encouraging others one-by-one. Are you willing to take the lead?

May this be the beginning of looking at the world as God intended and as He instructs us through His Word. May this be the beginning of reordering our personal values and motives, of reexamining how we use what God has entrusted to us. May this be the beginning of a new relationship with God and His creation as Christian stewards—a fresh understanding of the vital link God has designed between our possessions and our soul.

Questions for Group Discussion or Personal Reflection

CHAPTER ONE
1. After reading this chapter, do you really think God is watching how you use your stuff? Why or why not?
2. In Luke 16, why do you think God chooses to use a parable about a steward, or a financial manager? Why doesn't He just come out and tell us what to do?
3. Have you ever thought in terms of your possessions as being a tool? A test? A trademark?
4. How did you do on the take-home practice test (page 18)?
5. What lessons did you learn from taking the test?
6. Do you believe that God will really hold you accountable in heaven for how you use your stuff on earth?
7. Give some specific examples of ways that Christians can leverage possessions to build God's eternal kingdom.
8. Give some specific examples of ways you demonstrate your faith in the workplace by how you use your possessions.
9. How do your friends and neighbors know that you are a believer by observing your stuff (or lack thereof)?
10. As a result of reading this chapter, do you plan to make changes in your life? If so, what?

CHAPTER TWO

1. Do you believe that there is a direct link between how you use your possessions and your spiritual growth? If so, why?
2. Are you aware of anyone in your life who has modeled, or who currently models, this linkage of soul and stuff?
3. Do you think our culture is materialistic? If so, why, and what effect does it have on you?
4. Would you say that your life is things-centered or God-centered?
5. In reflecting on Mark Vincent's seven points of why money is godlike (page 26), what areas seem particularly true in your life?
6. Do you agree with Randy Alcorn's statement, "Our perspective on and handling of money is a litmus test of our true character. It is an index of our spiritual life"?
7. Do you believe it is possible to grow spiritually and form your soul? If so, how?
8. In the following formula, with what things do you agree or disagree? (1) Make all you can, (2) live as inexpensively as possible, and (3) provide maximum resources to God's kingdom work.
9. Did God make you to give? If so, why?
10. Does the pearl of great price apply in your life? If so, who is Lord of your life?

CHAPTER THREE

1. Do you agree or disagree with Donald Whitney's statement (page 39) that your giving reflects your obedience to Christ?
2. Do you agree or disagree with James Fowler's work (pages 40) that suggests there are stages of faith maturity? If so, why?
3. Which of Fowler's stages most accurately reflect where you are in your faith life?
4. Is it helpful in your Christian life to understand these stages of faith? If so, why?

5. Are you stuck and frustrated at a certain faith stage in your life?

6. What do you think about the corresponding correlation of soul maturity and the use of possessions? Is it an accurate assessment?

7. Does this correlation of faith maturity and how you use possessions hold true in your life? Why or why not?

8. Proposing that most Christians are in stage 3, the chapter states, "Convenience and relationships tend to shape their behavior rather than internalized convictions of faith." Do you agree?

9. Have you known (or do you currently know) anyone who exhibits the characteristics of stage 5 (generous) or stage 6 (mature steward)?

10. Do you desire to reach the top level of faith and use of possession stages? If so, what are you doing to get there?

CHAPTER FOUR

1. Do you know anyone like Paul Hubble (page 53), who has a biblical worldview of possessions? If so, do you know how he or she reached this level of maturity?

2. Do you agree with R. Scott Rodin's statement, "The concept of a godly steward is not an add-on to the 'proper' teaching on the life of the Christian, but instead it lies at its very heart." If so, why?

3. In your life, what are the main obstacles to becoming a faithful steward?

4. Have you ever taken the time to truly count your blessings, naming them one by one? Try it, as outlined in the chapter (page 56), and list what God has done.

5. Giving to God first is easy to say, but often the reality is very difficult to accomplish. What keeps you from giving to God first?

6. How do you think Paul's instruction in 2 Corinthians 8 (to give "according to your means") applies to you?

7. If "God loves a cheerful giver," are there examples in your life where you have given cheerfully?
8. Are you willing to give, regardless of your circumstances?
9. What do you think about tithing? Does it apply to you today? Why or why not?
10. If you want to become a faithful steward, list the ten principles outlined in this chapter, and then for each area, note specifically how you would implement these principles into your life.

CHAPTER FIVE

1. Do you think it is possible that you could learn from the lives of those who lived several hundred years ago? Why, or why not?
2. How can the plight of Anne Bradstreet be applied to your life today?
3. What do you think about the Keswick views: (1) that giving becomes a tool for the Christian to deepen his or her spiritual life; (2) that small things in our spiritual life are important; and (3) that we need to give our money and life completely to God? Does this apply today?
4. What are some of the main points about John Wesley's teaching on possessions (page 71) that seem relevant to you?
5. If John Wesley classified most American Christians in the 1700s as rich, what would he think about the church today?
6. Is "piling up wealth" incompatible with being a Christian?
7. Where would you draw the lines of acceptable wealth for a Christian?
8. What do you think about Charles Finney painting a picture of the Christian life as a "steady breaking free of the demands of the 'self' or the sinful nature?
9. Phoebe Palmer's writings chronicle the need for complete dedication to God (putting it all on the altar),

including the use of possessions. Have you read other authors who share this view? Does this concept apply today?

10. How do you relate to Hannah Whitall Smith's words, "We must no longer look upon our money as our own, but as belonging to the Lord, to be used in His service"?

11. If believers from the past knew a more excellent way, is it possible to live that way today?

CHAPTER SIX

1. Do you agree with Randy Alcorn's statement, "In the Christian community today, there is more blindness, rationalization, and unclear thinking about money than anything else"? Why or why not?

2. What do you think about the statement, "Just as today's culture has become more materialistic and has redefined itself without God, culture has also redefined our use of possessions without God"?

3. Does your experience validate a growing compartmentalization between your personal faith and your finances? What do you observe in the lives of others in the church?

4. Do you agree that our charity—what we do with our stuff—is inseparable from our culture, our character, and our soul?

5. Do you agree that our giving is motivated by: (1) how we benefit personally, or (2) a desire to help others, or (3) a desire to obey God as stewards?

6. Is it possible to live your life today embracing the biblical stewardship values: that God provides all, that God entrusts us as managers of these resources, and that God holds us accountable for how we manage these resources?

7. What is the difference between a steward (a servant of God) and a philanthropist (a friend of humankind)? Which concept motivates your giving?

8. Do you agree or disagree with the statement, "When philanthropy is motivated to help only people who

are a good business investment, charity becomes a form of exploitation"?

9. Do you agree with Robert Wuthnow's statement (page 91) that our attitude toward charitable giving allows us to carve up our caring into little chunks, which require only a level of giving that does not conflict with our needs and interests as individuals?

10. Are you on the wrong trail? Have you unknowingly been swallowed by the culture? Have you almost completely separated the way that you use your possessions from your spiritual life?

CHAPTER SEVEN

1. Do you agree with R. Scott Rodin's statement that "Giving is primarily a spiritual matter . . . an act of obedient worship . . . the spiritual growth of supporters should be the primary concern of every Christian fundraiser"?

2. Do you experience fund-raising activities to be primarily concerned with your spiritual growth? If not, why is this not the case?

3. Is your giving primarily impulsive or intentional? Why?

4. Considering how you currently give, does your system include the five-step giving paradigm described on page 96?

5. What particularly stood out as insightful and helpful in the five-step giving process?

6. In reviewing the five-step process, what steps are the most difficult for you to implement in your life?

7. In reviewing the nine expectations of Christian fundraisers (page 107), which stands out the most to you?

8. As you look over the eleven cautions in fund-raising appeals, which ones have you experienced, and how have they hindered your effort to grow spiritually through your giving?

9. What changes do you need to make in your life to become a more strategic steward?

10. Would you contact those organizations that you support and ask them to change the way that they approach you for finances, so that they support your spiritual formation?

Chapter Eight

1. In chapter 6, Francis Schaeffer suggests that, since the time of the Industrial Revolution, "The church was silent . . . on a compassionate use of wealth." How does your church do?

2. Do you agree or disagree with Robert Wuthnow's statement, "The doctrines of stewardship hold little meaning for many people. . . . there is a kind of mental or emotional gloss to contemporary religious teaching about money that prevents them from having much impact on how people actually live their lives"?

3. Does your pastor consistently integrate into his/her messages the concept that your giving is an important part of your spiritual life?

4. Does your church have a written philosophy about money and possessions? If not, would you be willing to help draft one?

5. When your church asks for money, is it done from a fund-raising perspective, or from a spiritual-growth perspective?

6. Why do you think churches, in general, are afraid to talk about money?

7. Does your church have a lay committee to oversee stewardship education? Are you willing to be personally involved in such a committee?

8. Are there methods of giving that your church could adopt that would facilitate your giving?

9. Would you be willing to publicly share your personal stewardship pilgrimage?

10. How can you pray (and for whom can you pray) for your church to strengthen its stewardship education program?

CHAPTER NINE

1. When you think back on your family life, do you remember receiving any instruction on biblical stewardship? Why, or why not?
2. Do you agree or disagree that the family should teach on stewardship through modeling and instruction?
3. As you consider modeling stewardship values, can you think of ways to accomplish this with children, other than the suggestions mentioned in the chapter?
4. Do you agree with the idea that you receive money by working? Why or why not is this an important concept?
5. If you are not making ends meet, should you generally try to make more, or spend less? Why?
6. Do you have any memories of how giving was so much a joy that you made it a habit?
7. In reviewing the possible expectations of Christian colleges, are you aware of any colleges or universities that take those expectations seriously?
8. Why do you think today's seminaries are extremely reluctant to take the lead in helping pastors and other church leaders to become better stewards?
9. Are you willing to contact colleges and seminaries that affect your life, and to encourage them to actively practice biblical stewardship?
10. Are you willing to make a change in your family's life, to change the cycle of teaching and modeling on stewardship?

CHAPTER TEN

1. Do you agree that if Christians were to turn the tide and grow biblical stewardship roots, the impact on the church and God's work would be immense, and transformation of lives would be profound? Why, or why not?
2. In your life, what will it take to respond to human need without discrimination, to make sacrifices for

others without concern for personal benefit, and to give glory to God?

3. If all of our resources (time, talents, and treasures) are not our own, how should this stewardship message change the way that we manage all of our lives?

4. As a Christian, do you really think that you are living in a hostile culture, trying to survive as a colony within an alien society? If so, how does that change what you do?

5. Are you living your life as someone who is just passing through earth, bound for heaven? Are you building rewards in heaven?

6. Do you feel a responsibility to share with others these biblical stewardship principles about your soul and your stuff?

7. Of the ten suggestions on ways to change (page 118), which two or three were most meaningful to you?

8. Considering where you are in your faith development, what next steps are you going to take to get your stuff in line with your soul?

9. Looking back through all the chapters of the book, what points do you see that were particularly meaningful in your spiritual journey?

10. Are you willing to join in consistent prayer with someone else, so that you can encourage each other in your faith walk, especially as it regards your stuff?

Notes

INTRODUCTION
1. Cynthia Heald, *Intimacy with God* (Colorado Springs: NavPress, 2000), p. 10.
2. Philip Yancey, *Money* (Portland, Ore.: Multnomah, 1985), p. 3.
3. Randy Alcorn, *Money, Possessions, and Eternity* (Wheaton, Ill.: Tyndale, 1989), preface.
4. Robert Wuthnow, *God and Mammon in America* (New York: Free Press, 1994), p. 151.
5. Larry Burkett, *The Word on Finances* (Chicago: Moody, 1994).
6. Dallas Willard, in Walt Russell's *Playing with Fire* (Colorado Springs: NavPress, 2000), p. 11.

CHAPTER 1: GOD'S MAP FOR YOUR STUFF AND YOUR SOUL
1. Gary L. Thomas, *The Glorious Pursuit: Embracing the Virtues of Christ* (Colorado Springs: NavPress, 1998), p. 108.
2. Dallas Willard, *The Divine Conspiracy: Rediscovering Our Hidden Life in God* (San Francisco: Harper Collins, 1998).
3. Andy Stanley, "Seeing as God Sees," address to Christian Stewardship Association Conference (Atlanta, Ga., September 29, 2000).
4. Randy Alcorn, *Money, Possessions, and Eternity* (Wheaton, Ill.: Tyndale, 1989), p. 22.
5. Bruce Wilkinson, *Walk Thru Eternal Rewards* seminar notebook, *Walk Thru the Bible* (Atlanta, Ga., 2000).

6. Brian Kluth, *The Word for the Wealthy* (Colorado Springs: Kingdom Seekers, 2000).
7. Based on personal interview with Brian Kluth, April, 1999.
8. Bruce Demarest, *Satisfy Your Soul* (Colorado Springs: NavPress, 1999).

CHAPTER 2: SPIRITUAL GROWTH AND YOUR STUFF

1. Randy Alcorn, *Money, Possessions, and Eternity* (Wheaton, Ill.: Tyndale House, 1989), pp. 21-22.
2. Mark Vincent, *A Christian View of Money* (Scottdale, Pa.: Herald Press, 1984), p. 22.
3. C. S. Lewis, *The Screwtape Letters* (New York: Macmillan, 1951), p. 143.
4. A. W. Tozer, *The Pursuit of God* (Harrisburg, Pa.: Christian Publications, 1958), p. 22.
5. Craig Blomberg, *Neither Poverty nor Riches: A Biblical Theology of Material Possessions* (Grand Rapids, Mich.: Eerdmans, 1999).
6. Oprah Winfrey's summary for the television theme "Remembering your Spirit," http://www.oprah.com/rys/discovmain.htm.
7. J. P. Moreland, *Love Your God with All Your Mind: The Role of Reason in the Life of the Soul* (Colorado Springs: NavPress, 1997), p. 69.
8. Reinhardt Grossmann, *The Existence of the World: An Introduction to Ontology* (London: Routledge, 1994).
9. Literal translation from McReynolds; Paul R., *Nestle Aland 26th Edition Greek New Testament with McReynolds English Interlinear* (Oak Harbor, Wash.: Logos Research Systems, Inc. 1997).
10. http://www.greenville.edu/publications/mannoia-texts/mannoia5499chapel.shtml
11. Dallas Willard, *Spirit of the Disciplines* (San Francisco: Harper & Row, 1988), ch. 9.
12. Richard Foster in Dallas Willard, *Spirit of the Disciplines* (San Francisco: Harper & Row, 1988), p. 26.

13. Gerhard Kittel and Gerhard Friedrich, eds., *The Theological Dictionary of the New Testament*, Abridged in One Volume (Grand Rapids, Mich.: Eerdmans, 1985).

14. Kittel and Friedrich.

15. John Piper, *Desiring God* (Portland, Oreg.: Multnomah, 1996), p. 170.

16. Piper, p. 163.

CHAPTER 3: MARKS OF A MATURE STEWARD

1. Donald S. Whitney, *Spiritual Disciplines for the Christian Life* (Colorado Springs: NavPress, 1991), p. 140.

2. Randy Alcorn, *Money, Possessions, and Eternity* (Wheaton, Ill.: Tyndale, 1989), p. 18.

3. M. Scott Peck quoted from James W. Fowler's *Stages of Faith* (San Francisco: Harper Collins, 1995).

4. James W. Fowler, *Stages of Faith* (San Francisco: Harper Collins, 1995), p. xii.

5. Fowler, p. 122.

6. Thomas Schmidt, "Rich Wisdom: New Testament Teachings on Wealth," *Christianity Today* (May 12, 1989), p. 30.

7. P. H. McNamara, "What People Give Indicates Their Spiritual Health," in *More Than Money: Portraits of Transformative Stewardship* (Bethesda, Md.: The Alban Institute, 1999).

8. Based on personal interview with Dave Adrian, July, 2000.

9. Gary L. Thomas, *The Glorious Pursuit: Embracing the Virtues of Christ* (Colorado Springs: NavPress, 1998), p. 108.

10. Based on personal interview with Dave Beckman, March, 2000.

11. Story adapted from *Mission Frontiers* (Sept./Oct., 1994, No. 9-10), pp. 23-24.

12. *Mission Frontiers*, pp. 23-24.

CHAPTER 4: HOW THEN SHALL YOU BECOME A
FAITHFUL STEWARD?
1. Ronald Vallet, "The Church, Its Mission, and Its
   Funding," *Journal of Stewardship*, (Indianapolis:
   Ecumenical Center for Stewardship Studies, 1994).
2. Based on personal interview with Paul Hubble,
   October, 2000.
3. R. Scott Rodin, *Stewards in the Kingdom* (Downers
   Grove, Ill.: InterVarsity, 2000), p. 186.
4. Johnson Oatman, Jr., "Count Your Blessings," from
   The Hymnal for Worship and Celebration, (Waco,
   Tex.: Word Music, 1996), no. 562.
5. Ron W. Blue, *Generous Living: Finding Contentment
   Through Giving* (Grand Rapids, Mich.: Zondervan,
   1997), p. 37.
6. *Crown Ministries Small Group Financial Study*
   (Longwood, Fla.: Crown Ministries, 1986), p. 37.
7. Daniel Kadlec, "Get Out of Hock," *Time* (May 22,
   2000).
8. Larry Eskridge, "When Burkett Speaks, Evangelicals
   Listen," *Christianity Today* (July 12, 2000).
9. Howard Dayton, *Your Money Counts: The Biblical
   Guide to Earning, Spending, Saving, Investing,
   Giving, and Getting Out of Debt* (Longwood, Fla.:
   Crown Ministries, 1996).
10. Randy Alcorn, *Money, Possessions, and Eternity*
    (Wheaton, Ill.: Tyndale, 1989), p. 217.

CHAPTER 5: LESSONS FROM EARLIER CHRISTIANS
1. Jeannine Hensley, ed., "Here follows some verses
   upon the burning of our house, July 10th, 1666,"
   Works of Anne Bradstreet (Cambridge, Mass.: The
   John Harvard Library, 1981).
2. Evan C. Hopkins, ed., *The Keswick Week*, 1898
   (London: Marshall Brothers, 1898), p. 27.
3. Hopkins, p. 30.
4. Hopkins, p. 30.

5. Hopkins, p. 19.
6. Hopkins, p. 51.
7. Hopkins, p. 78.
8. This and other details of this paragraph can be found in Steven Barabas, *So Great Salvation: the History and Message of the Keswick Convention* (London: Marshall, Morgan & Scott, 1952), pp. 151-152.
9. Hopkins, p. 190.
10. Hopkins, p. 177.
11. John Wesley, *The Bicentennial Edition of the Works of John Wesley vol. 2*, ed. Frank Baker (Nashville, Abingdon, 1985).
12. Wesley, p. 268.
13. Wesley, p. 268.
14. Wesley, p. 274.
15. Wesley, p. 274.
16. Wesley, p. 276.
17. Wesley, pp. 283-284.
18. Wesley, p. 277.
19. *Works of John Wesley, vol. 3*, p. 230.
20. Wesley, p. 229.
21. Wesley, p. 233.
22. Wesley, pp. 267-275.
23. Charles G. Finney, *Lectures to Professing Christians* (New York: Garland Publishing, Inc., 1985), p. 95.
24. Finney, p. 96.
25. Thomas C. Oden, ed., *Phoebe Palmer: Selected Writings* (New York: Paulist Press, 1988), p. 198.
26. Oden, p. 100.
27. Hannah Whitall Smith, *The Christian's Secret of a Happy Life* (Westwood, N.J.: Revell, 1952), p. 211.
28. Smith, p. 200.

CHAPTER 6: HOW DID WE GET HERE?
1. Randy Alcorn, *Money, Possessions, and Eternity* (Wheaton, Ill.: Tyndale, 1989), p. 27.
2. Nathan Hatch, "Can Evangelicalism Survive Its Success?", *Christianity Today* (October 5, 1992) p. 36,

and Mark Noll, *A History of Christianity in the United States and Canada* (Grand Rapids, Mich.: Eerdmans, 1993).

3. David Wells, "Lengthening Shadows and Peril Over Evangelicalism" at the annual convention of the National Association of Evangelicals, 1992.

4. John and Sylvia Ronsvalle, *Behind the Stained Glass Windows* (Grand Rapids, Mich.: Baker, 1996).

5. John and Sylvia Ronsvalle, *The State of Church Giving through 1998* (Champaign, Ill.: Empty Tomb, Inc., 2000).

6. Robert Payton, "God and Money," in D. F. Burlingame, ed., *The Responsibilities of Wealth* (Bloomington, Ind.: Indiana University Press, 1992); Robert Wuthnow, "Pious Materialism: How Americans View Faith and Money," *The Christian Century* (March 3, 1993); Robert Wuthnow, Virginia A. Hodgkinson, and Associates, *Faith and Philanthropy in America* (San Francisco: Jossey-Bass, 1990).

7. George Barna, *The Mind of the Donor* (Glendale Calif.: Barna Research Group, 1994).

8. David L. McKenna, "Giving Is Not Guaranteed," keynote speech to Christian Stewardship Association, September 20, 1992, Indianapolis, Ind.

9. Peter Dobkin Hall, *Inventing the Nonprofit Sector* (Baltimore, Md.: Johns Hopkins University Press, 1992).

10. Nathan Hatch, *The Democratization of American Christianity in the United States and Canada* (New Haven: Yale University Press, 1989), p. 53.

11. Alexis de Tocqueville, *Democracy in America,* (1835; reprint, New York: New American Library, 1956).

12. Andrew Carnegie, *The Gospel of Wealth and Other Timely Essays,* (Cambridge: Belknap Press of Harvard University Press, 1962), p. 29.

13. Peter Dobkin Hall, p. 40.

14. Charles M. Sheldon, *In His Steps,* (Springdale, Pa.: Whitaker House, 1897).

15. Francis Schaeffer, *How Shall We Then Live? The Rise and Decline of Western Thought and Culture* (Old Tappan, N.J.: Revell, 1976), p. 114.

16. Robert D. Noles, *Water Boy!* (Glendale, Calif.: Church Press, 1984).

17. Robert Goheen, quoted from David McKenna's "Giving Is Not Guaranteed," keynote speech to Christian Stewardship Association, September 20, 1992, Indianapolis, Ind.

18. Robert Wuthnow, *Acts of Compassion* (Princeton, N.J.: Princeton University Press, 1991), p. 88.

19. Wuthnow, "Pious Materialism: How Americans View Faith and Money."

20. Robert Payton, "God and Money," from *The Responsibilities of Wealth*, p. 34.

21. Jacob Riis, *How the Other Half Lives* (1892; reprint, New York: Sagamore Press, 1957), pp. 198-199.

22. Hall, p. 133.

23. Hall, p. 184.

24. Hall, p. 184.

CHAPTER 7: WHEN EVERYONE HAS THEIR HANDS OUT

1. R. Scott Rodin, *Stewards in the Kingdom: A Theology of Life in All Its Fullness* (Downers Grove, Ill.: InterVarsity, 2000).

2. Alan Youngren, "On Becoming a Strategic Steward," from *Money for Ministries*, Wesley K. Willmer, ed. (Wheaton, Ill.: Victor, 1989).

3. E. J. Hales and A. Youngren, *Your Money, Their Ministry: A Guide to Responsible Christian Giving* (Grand Rapids, Mich.: Eerdmans, 1981).

4. Harold Seymour, *Designs for Fund-Raising* (New York: McGraw-Hill, 1966).

5. Wesley K. Willmer and J. David Schmidt with Martyn Smith, *The Prospering Parachurch* (San Francisco: Jossey-Bass, 1998).

6. *Didache.*

7. R. Scott Rodin, *Stewards in the Kingdom.*

8. Thomas H. Jeavons and Rebekah Burch Basinger, *Growing Givers' Hearts: Treating Fundraising as Ministry* (San Francisco: Jossey-Bass, 2000).

Chapter 8: What You Should Expect from Your Church

1. *The Reluctant Steward*, A Report and Commentary on the Stewardship and Development Study (Indianapolis and St. Meinrad, Ind.: Christian Theological Seminary and Saint Meinrad Seminary, 1992).

2. Robert Wuthnow, *The Crisis in the Church: Spiritual Malaise, Financial Woe* (New York: Oxford University Press, 1997).

3. Wuthnow, *God and Mammon in America* (New York: Free Press, 1994).

4. John and Sylvia Ronsvalle, *Behind the Stained Glass Window: Money Dynamics in the Church* (Grand Rapids, Mich.: Baker Books, 1996), p. 3.

5. Brian Kluth, *Maximum Generosity Church Resource Guide* (Colorado Springs: Kingdom Seekers, 2000).

6. Kennon L. Callahan, *Effective Church Finances* (San Francisco: Jossey-Bass, 1992), p. 5.

7. Dean Hoge, Patrick McNamara, Charles Zech, *Plain Talk About Churches and Money* (Bethesda, Md.: The Alban Institute, 1997).

8. George Barna, *How to Increase Giving in Your Church* (Ventura, Calif.: Regal, 1997), p. 7.

9. Michael Durall, *Creating Congregations of Generous People* (Bethesda, Md.: The Alban Institute, 1999), p. 12.

Chapter 9: What Families and Educators Should Be Doing

1. Thomas H. Jeavons and Rebekah Burch Basinger, *Growing Givers' Hearts: Treating Fundraising as Ministry* (San Francisco: Jossey-Bass, 2000).

2. Randy Alcorn, *Money, Possessions, and Eternity* (Wheaton, Ill.: Tyndale, 1989), p. 18.

3. L. Eskridge and M. Noll, eds., *More Money, More Ministry: Money and Evangelicals in Recent North American History* (Grand Rapids, Mich.: Eerdmans, 2000).

4. Bander Family, personal interview, January 2001.
5. Morris Family, personal interview, January 2001.
6. John Coe, "Intentional Spiritual Formation in the Classroom: Making Space for the Spirit in the University," *Christian Educational Journal* 4 NS (2000), p. 85-110.
7. Coe.

CHAPTER 10: KEEPING YOUR SOUL ALIVE

1. Russell Chandler, *Racing Toward 2001: The Forces Shaping America's Religious Future* (Grand Rapids, Mich.: Zondervan, 1992), p. 220.
2. Robert Payton, "God and Money," from *The Responsibilities of Wealth*, D. F. Burlingame, ed., (Bloomington, Ind.: Indiana University Press, 1992), p. 139.
3. G. Blumenstyk, "Charitable Giving Trailed Inflation Again in 1993, But Education Fared Better Than Most Causes," *Chronicle of Higher Education* (June 1, 1994), p. A23.
4. Yankelovich, Skelly, and White, *The Charitable Behavior of Americans* (Washington, D.C.: Independent Sector, 1986), and V. A. Hodgkinson and M. S. Weitzman, *Giving and Volunteering in the United States* (Washington, D.C.: Independent Sector, 1994).
5. J. White, *The Church and the Parachurch: An Uneasy Marriage* (Portland, Ore.: Multnomah, 1983), p. 8.
6. George Barna, *The Mind of the Donor* (Glendale, Calif.: Barna Research Group, 1994), p. 42.
7. John and Sylvia Ronsvalle, *The State of Church Giving through 1998* (Champaign, Ill.: Empty Tomb, Inc., 2000), p. 23.
8. S. Hart, "Religious Giving: Patterns and Variations," paper presented at the annual meetings of the Religious Research Association and the Society for the Scientific Study of Religion (Virginia Beach, Va.: November 9, 1990).
9. Barna, p. 56.

10. David McKenna, "Giving Is Not Guaranteed," keynote speech to Christian Stewardship Association, September 20, 1992, Indianapolis, Ind.
11. *The Reluctant Steward*, A Report and Commentary on the Stewardship and Development Study (Indianapolis and St. Meinrad, IN: Christian Theological Seminary and Saint Meinrad Seminary, 1992).
12. Stanley Hauerwas and William Willimon, *Resident Aliens* (Nashville: Abingdon, 1989), p. 15.
13. James Davison Hunter, *Evangelicalism: The Coming Generation* (Chicago: The University of Chicago Press, 1987).
14. Waldo Werning, *Supply-Side Stewardship* (St. Louis: Concordia, 1992), p. 48.
15. Robert Wuthnow, "Pious Materialism: How Americans View Faith and Money," *The Christian Century* (March 3, 1993).
16. Hunter, *Evangelicalism: The Coming Generation*, p. 139.
17. Barna.
18. Robert Bellah, *Habits of the Heart* (Berkeley, Calif.: University of California Press, 1985), p. 51.
19. Robert Bellah, *The Good Society* (New York: Vintage Books, 1992), p. 73.
20. Max DePree, *Leadership Is an Art* (New York: Bantam, Doubleday, Dell, 1992).
21. Timothy Smith, *Revivalism and Social Reform* (New York: Harper & Row, 1965).
22. Quoted in "Stewardship and Almsgiving" by William E. McManus in *Faith and Philanthropy in America*, ed., Robert Wuthnow, Virginia A. Hodgkinson, and Associates (San Francisco: Jossey-Bass, 1990).

Authors

WESLEY K. WILLMER IS VICE PRESIDENT OF UNIVERSITY Advancement and a professor at Biola University in La Mirada, California, with responsibility for enrollment management, alumni, marketing communications, development, intercollegiate athletics, and university planning. His career in Christian higher education has included serving at Seattle Pacific University, Roberts Wesleyan College, the Billy Graham Center, and Wheaton College. From 1986–1996, he served on the board of the Christian Stewardship Association, serving as chairperson the last four years.

In 1987 he initiated and directed the national conference "Funding the Christian Challenge," which attracted nationwide media attention in such publications as *Christianity Today, U. S. News and World Report, Fund Raising Management,* and *The Washington Post.* He has initiated and obtained grants of more than $1 million to study and improve nonprofit/faith-based management practices.

In addition to addressing various conferences and consulting with nonprofit organizations, he has been author, coauthor, editor, or editor-in-chief of twenty books and many professional journal publications. One recent book is *The Prospering Parachurch: Enlarging the Boundaries of God's Kingdom,* published by Jossey-Bass. *Fund Raising Management* magazine selected him to write on the future of funding religion for its 25th anniversary issue. He is also on the editorial board of *Boardwise.*

In 1986 the Council for Advancement and Support of Education selected Willmer from among its 14,000 individual members at more than 2,800 institutions to receive its annual award for significant contributions in research and writing. In 1993 he was chosen from the same membership to serve on the National Commission on Philanthropy, and in 1999 he was asked to serve on the editorial board of *CASE International Journal of Educational Advancement*. In 1999 the Christian Stewardship Association honored him as the 1999 Outstanding Stewardship Professional. His alma mater selected him as one of one hundred "alumni of a growing vision" out of the more than 40,000 alumni.

Willmer earned a B.A. in psychology and an M.Ed. in counseling and guidance at Seattle Pacific University. His Ph.D. in higher education was granted by the State University of New York at Buffalo. He resides in Fullerton, California, with his wife, Sharon. They have three grown children: J. Brian (wife Lindsay), A. Kristell, and Stephen.

$ $ $ $ $ $

MARTYN SMITH IS A FREELANCE WRITER AND A FREQUENT presenter of seminars on religious and literary topics. He holds a Master of Theology degree from Fuller Theological Seminary, where the faculty awarded him the American Bible Society Scholarly Achievement Award for Old Testament. He is a doctoral student in comparative literature at Emory University.